The
Rottweiler
Handbook

Joan Hustace Walker

With Full-color Photographs

BARRON'S

About the Author

Joan Hustace Walker has been writing professionally since 1984. She is a member of the Authors Guild, the American Society of Journalists and Authors, the Dog Writers Association of America, the Cat Writers Association, and the Society of Environmental Journalists. Walker writes for both general and technical audiences, specializing in animals, education, aging, and environmental issues. Her other book titles include *St. Bernards, Old English Sheepdogs, Great Pyrenees,* and the *Boxer Handbook.* She has had more than 200 articles published by a variety of magazines, including *Modern Maturity, Family Circle,* and *Dog World* and has been awarded multiple "Maxwell Awards" by the Dog Writers Association of America.

Photo Credits

Curtis Hustace: pages 4, 5, 7, 8, 12, 14, 15, 17, 18, 22, 25, 26, 29, 32, 36, 37, 40, 42, 44, 46, 47, 48, 55, 62, 64, 65, 67, 69, 73, 75, 78, 79, 82, 83, 85, 88, 89, 91, 93, 97, 98, 101, 103, 104, 105, 110, 113, 114, 116, 119, 121, 122, 126, 127, 128, 130, 131, 132, 135, 137, 140, 141, 142, 143, 144, 145, 146, 147, 149, 151, 153, 154, 163; Dr. and Mrs. Karl W. Rice: pages 13, 102, 150 (photographer Jerry Vavra), 157, 165; Joan Hustace Walker: pages 23, 161; Steve Paschkewitz: pages 60, 71.

Cover Photos

Curtis Hustace.

All inquiries should be addressed to:
Barron's Educational Series, Inc.
250 Wireless Boulevard
Hauppauge, New York 11788
http://www.barronseduc.com

International Standard Book No. 0-7641-1642-8

Library of Congress Catalog Card No. 00-067615

Library of Congress Cataloging-in-Publication Data
Walker, Joan Hustace, 1962–
          The Rottweiler handbook / Joan Hustace Walker.
     p.   cm.
     Includes bibliographical references (p.).
     ISBN 0-7641-1642-8
     1. Rottweiler dog. I. Title.

SF429.R7 W35   2001
636.73—dc21   00-067615

Printed in China

Important Note

This pet handbook gives advice to the reader about buying and caring for a new dog. The author and the publisher consider it important to point out that the advice given in the book applies to normally developed puppies or adult dogs, obtained from recognized dog breeders or adoption shelters, dogs that have been examined and are in excellent health with good temperament.

Anyone who adopts a grown dog should be aware that the animal has already formed its basic knowledge of human beings and their customs. The new owner should watch the animal carefully, especially its attitude and behavior toward humans. If possible, the new owner should meet the former owners before adopting the dog. If the dog comes from a shelter, the new owner should make an effort to obtain information about the dog's background, temperament, and peculiarities. Dogs that come from abusive homes or from homes in which they have been treated abnormally may react to handling in an unnatural manner, and may have a tendency to snap or bite. Dogs with this nature should only be adopted by people who have had experience with such dogs.

Caution is further advised in the association of children with dogs, both puppies and adults, and in meeting other dogs, whether on or off lead.

Well-behaved and carefully supervised dogs may cause damage to someone else's property or cause accidents. It is therefore in the owner's interest to be adequately insured against such eventualities, and we strongly urge all dog owners to purchase a liability policy that covers their dog.

Contents

Acknowledgments

This book would not have been possible without the kind and generous help of many Rottweiler breeders, trainers, and owners both in the United States and in Germany. I would like to express my deepest appreciation to German Rottweiler fanciers Anton Spindler and Franz Menacher for taking hours of their time to talk with me in depth about the German Rottweiler, and introducing me to their wonderful dogs, and to Gabriele Tenscher for sharing her training skills. Also, a special thank you to Dr. Manfred Herrmann, president of the ADRK, who was integral in supplying me with historical information on the breed and putting me in contact with Rottweiler breeders. Additionally, I would be remiss in not acknowledging the tireless efforts of Heinrich Mörtl, Christine Hupmann, and Petra Kulp in translating interviews, correspondence, and materials for me in Germany and in the United States.

Among the American Rottweiler fanciers, there are many owners, breeders, and trainers I have talked with throughout the past year who have all contributed information and tips for this book. However, I would like to especially express my gratitude to Donna Rice, Barb McNinch, and Joan Sweeney for talking endlessly with me about all facets of the Rottweiler and for painstakingly reviewing every line of the manuscript for this book. They are all outstanding experts who epitomize responsible Rottweiler breeders, owners, rescuers, and trainers, and without their input and critical reviews, I would not have been able to represent this magnificent breed in such a true light.

And, of course, a big thank you to Rottweiler breeder and rescue founder, Frank Wilkins, who was the first to say, "You should write a book on Rottweilers," and who has been an endless source of Rottweiler information and support for this book. In large part, he has ingrained in me a permanent appreciation and love for this tremendous breed.

Chapter One
History of the Rottweiler

The wind is blowing from the southwest today, picking up a cold sting from the rolling Swabian Mountains. Dressed warmly, for a misty rain is beginning to fall, the stalwart butcher watches carefully as his dogs work to keep a dozen restless cattle together along this worn valley road. The cattle are from the Neckar River Valley, having been purchased two days prior, and are headed to Rottweil to be butchered. With only his two dogs as help, the butcher is well aware that herding even this small, jittery group of cattle is a formidable task and one that can be fraught with dangers.

A step ahead of his master, the larger of the two dogs has already spotted and marked his challenge. An older steer, the leader of this group of cattle, is nervous and considering bolting from the herd. Without control of this steer, the entire herd can fall to pieces and scatter within seconds. Quickly and without a sound, the dog boldly confronts the steer, face to face, staying but a yard or so away from the animal's horns. The steer lowers his head and shakes it threateningly, blowing loudly from his flared nostrils. The dog lowers his head and shoulders slightly and returns a steely glare.

It is a battle of wills, with the steer outweighing the canine by close to a thousand pounds. The dog charges at the menacing steer, both to enforce his point and cement his position as the leader of this herd. Meanwhile, the other dog works the far side of the herd, keeping the cattle moving together and forward as a group. The challenging steer finally acquiesces to the dog, deciding it is better not to deal with what this dog might do, and reenters the herd. With the ringleader in control, the dogs now have command of the entire herd and the cattle move a little less nervously along the road.

The lead dog casts a quick eye back at his master. A nod and a grunt of approval are all that are needed for reassurance of a job well done, and the butcher's dogs go back to their silent trotting alongside the herd, keeping an ever-watchful and keen eye for trouble. Not only must the dogs keep the cattle herd together and calm, they must also protect the herd and their master from robbers and wolves along the way.

What Is the Rottweiler?

What is this dog that performs time-honored duties with great perfection? What is this dog that possesses the cleverness, intuition, and confidence necessary to master cattle herds over great distances, and is equally as willing to pull a cart loaded with goods or slaughtered meat to market? It is, of course, the butcher's dog of Rottweil, a dog so highly esteemed in medieval days, that citizens were jailed for stealing the butcher's dog. Most notably, in 1468 two citizens, who reportedly were caught stealing a butcher's Rottweiler, were forced to appear before the Archduchess Mechthild in Rottenburg, Germany.

Of course, stealing a dog wasn't the only crime that was punishable when it came to Rottweilers in those days; mistreating or not properly caring for a Rottweiler was enough to create serious repercussions for the dog owner. In 1669 a member of Rottweil's town council was forced to resign because he did not treat his dog—a Rottweiler—properly.

On a more humorous note, the Stadtarchiv Rottweil reveals that the mayor of Rottweil in 1504, Heinrich Freyburger, bought lottery tickets for his dogs, Weidmann, and Pratsch. Though the records don't reveal whether Herr Freyburger's Rottweilers actually won any money or not, without a doubt these dogs were highly valued. Rottweilers, in general, were largely integral to the success of the citizens and Rottweil itself.

Early History

In a land edged by the Alps to the south and the Black Forest to the west, the town of Rottweil is credited with developing the breed known as the Rottweiler. The dog's adeptness at herding and driving cattle and sheep, as well as his ability to guard livestock and the butcher's money from thieves (the dog would wear the purse filled with money around its neck), quickly gained him recognition in surrounding cities and countries. In Rottweil itself, the dog was referred to as simply "the butcher's dog" or "Metzgerhund"; however, people from other areas soon began to identify the sturdy and intelligent dog with his origins. Thus, the butcher's dog became "the dog from Rottweil," or "Rottweiler."

The Romans

Though the Rottweiler is perhaps most famous for his centuries of cattle work from the Middle Ages to the mid-nineteenth century, the Rottweiler's origins and working abilities are thought to possibly date back to the Romans.

In 73 A.D. the Roman Legate Cnaeus Cornelius Pinarius Clemens established a military camp in the area of what is today Rottweil. Working their way up from Vindonissa,

Because dogs were not bred as "purebreds" until the late 1800s in Europe, the Rottweiler did not consistently resemble the breed we recognize today until the early 1900s.

Switzerland, Roman troops built roads from Switzerland, up along the Rhine River to Brig, Germany, and finally into Rottweil. The encampment is thought to have been a substantial one, since the Romans erected at least five castles in the area.

In Roman days, food was "on the hoof"—livestock to feed the vast Roman armies were cared for by the troops and traveled with the men. Dogs that could effectively herd and drive cattle as well as guard the livestock were highly valued by the Romans, and traveled with the troops as working dogs. The Romans' herding dogs are thought to have been swift, somewhat large and strong, and possessing the athleticism, courage, and tenacity to herd cattle. At least some of the progenitors of today's Rottweiler are believed to have come from the large Mastiff-type dogs that originally accompanied these Roman troops to this location.

The Roman's military camp on the Neckar River soon became a town, or "Municipium," which is a Roman city according to Italian law. Between 81 and 96 A.D. the town was named Arae Flaviae, and was to become the main administrative center for the Romans east of the Rhine River. The town, which had been originally constructed of wood, flourished and was rebuilt with stone buildings to match its rising importance. Arae Flaviae boasted three Gallo-Roman temples, three public baths, and large blocks of stone houses. During this time, it is generally assumed that the Romans' dogs were bred with local herding dogs.

By 260 A.D. the Romans left the area. Arae Flaviae may have been destroyed, or it may have been attacked by the Alemans, a tribe of Germanic people living in that area. The exact cause for the departure of the Romans from the city is not known with certainty, but it is generally assumed that not all of the Romans' herding dogs returned with their original owners, and that many of the dogs' progeny remained in the area with local citizens. The Alemans settled on the edge of the old Roman city and developed a town that in time would flourish.

Canine Influences

Exactly what canine influences may have entered the picture over the next 1,000 years in developing or transforming the Roman's cattle herding and guarding dogs into today's Rottweiler is a subject of much debate. One theory is that Swiss cattle herding dogs, such as the Bernese Mountain Dog, had an influence on the developing breed. This is not without possibility, given the location and later importance of Rottweil as a trade center for cattle, as well as its close association with Switzerland.

Another theory is that a breed of dog originating in Belgium, the Bra-

banter Bullenbeisser, may have had some influence on the development of the Rottweiler during the Middle Ages. The Brabanter Bullenbeisser, which is now extinct, had been used by noblemen in southern Germany to hunt wild boar.

What is known of these centuries of the "early" Rottweiler, is that breeders in those days were not searching for any ideal shape, color, or form, or attempting to develop a certain breed; what the butcher wanted was simply the best working dog possible. Color was of little importance, and form mattered in only a functional sense—the dog must be athletic and its physical shape must help, not hinder, the dog's working performance. As for temperament, a nervous or timid dog simply would not do when it came to herding cattle and guard work. A calm, confident temperament, however, was ideal.

The Town of Rottweil

By the late 700s A.D. the town that had once been known as Arae Flaviae by the Romans, had become known by its new inhabitants as Rotuvilla, and later Rottweil. As Rottweil, the town flourished again. It had a King's Court that was tasked with looking after an administrative district for Charles the Great. By the mid-1200s Rottweil was considered one of the most important cities in what was then known as Swabia, a country that included parts of France and Switzerland, as well as this area of Germany. By 1378 Rottweil became a "free city," with its own constitution. It is at this time that Rottweil established itself as a trading post for cattle and cereals, and continued to be a leading town in southern Germany for centuries.

During the 1400s, Rottweil was the seat of an imperial court, which had a district at the time extending from Cologne, Germany, to Central Switzerland. During the fifteenth century Rottweil entered into an "Eternal Union" with the Swiss Confederation. With a background of such independence and confidence, it is no small wonder that the Rottweiler today mirrors some of the admirable qualities of the citizens' themselves!

Loss of Work for the Rottweiler

In the mid-1800s, the Rottweiler suddenly found himself out of the cattle-herding business. With the advent of the railroad and a more efficient means of transporting cattle, the demand for the Rottweiler as a working dog fell dramatically. A law was also passed at this time forbidding driving cattle over roads, further reducing the need for this great cattle-herding dog.

With no job, the working Rottweiler reportedly nearly became extinct by the end of the nineteenth century. Fortunately, at this same time, German breeders showed renewed interest in the breed and organized an International Club for Leonberger and Rottweiler Dogs. A breed standard was written in 1883

Red Stones

Though many books claim the town of Rottweil was named for its red tile roofs, historians Hartwig Ebert and Winfried Hecht, suggest otherwise. According to Ebert and Hecht, the town of Rottweil was originally called Rotuvilla, a name that first appeared in writing in 771 A.D. The name Rotuvilla does not refer to red tile roofs; rather, historians say that the name refers to the massive red stones used by the Romans to build homes, temples, and public baths in and around the area.

From the town hall in Rottweil, the Oberbürgermeister (Mayor) of Rottweil continues to serve as a signing authority for the ADRK (Rottweiler Club of Germany).

by Albert Kull and published by the club in 1901.

The First Standard

Interestingly, the first Rottweiler standard shows that the breed had much more variation that it would even 20 years later. It included the color scheme of today (black with rust to mahogany markings), but also included brindle on gray with fawn markings, red fawn with a black nose with fawn markings, and a dark gray with a black saddle and head with fawn markings. The standard also noted that some white markings (chest and legs) were allowable and occurred frequently.

The First Clubs

The first club exclusively for Rottweilers, the Deutsche Rottweiler Club, was formed in January 1907, shortly after the Leonberger and Rottweiler club failed. Between 1907 and 1921 two more clubs would be formed: the South German Rottweiler Club, and the International Rottweiler Club (IRC), which later absorbed the South German Rottweiler Club. A breed standard published in 1913 by the IRC no longer recognized the brindle variation or gray wolf coloring, but did include black and brown with the classic Rottweiler markings, as well as blue,

---

Burning Question

Any guess as to what breed the fire station mascot in Rottweil, Germany, is? The Rottweiler, of course!

---

and red with a black mask and line down the back.

In 1921 the two clubs merged to form the Allgemeiner Deutscher Rottweiler Klub (ADRK), which is now Germany's Rottweiler club. At the time of the ADRK's formation, a new standard allowed only black coloration with the classic rust to mahogany markings. White markings on the chest and underside were allowed, but not desirable.

The Rottweiler's present and future are still deeply rooted in southern Germany in the Rottweiler's ancestral town of Rottweil. The Oberbürgermeister of Rottweil's official duties include serving as the signing authority for the ADRK. The Oberbürgermeister is not merely a figurehead for "show," but is an active, participating member of the Rottweiler club and the breed's future.

Development of the Breed in Germany

As the potential for dogs serving in police work was realized, Germany began developing a police dog program and in 1910 the German Police Dog Association accepted the Rottweiler as a working police dog. It was the fourth breed to be accepted, following German Shepherd Dogs, Doberman Pinschers, and Airedale Terriers. This event is credited with stoking interest and perhaps even saving the Rottweiler as a breed.

World War I

In 1914 World War I broke out and dogs that were qualified as police dogs were called up for military duty. The German forces reportedly fielded a canine corps numbering in the thousands. Rottweilers were among those that served valiantly in this war. War dogs were not, however, used solely as patrol dogs or as watchdogs at POW camps, though there were dogs that served in these capacities. Some of the more interesting jobs included detection dogs, which were trained to growl softly if they detected movement on the Allied forces' side, and messenger dogs, or couriers, dogs that were specially trained to carry messages in tubes attached to their collars. Messenger dogs traveled silently over long distances and through war-ravaged land.

Dogs in the canine corps were also called upon to carry spools of unwinding telephone wire from one point to another, avoiding bullets and mines and negotiating shelled-out terrain along the way. Ambulance or medic dogs were taught to seek out wounded soldiers, return to a medic, and then lead the medic back to the wounded soldier.

Rottweilers that were called up to serve suffered great losses. As a matter of pride and great respect for their country, many German breeders gave some of their very finest Rottweilers for service in the war. Many of these dogs died and their potential progeny were lost forever.

The Rottweiler was one of the first breeds to be certified as a police dog in Germany and continues to be one of the finest working breeds in the world.

Historical accounts show that life was also difficult for dogs that did not "serve." Breeders with dogs at home experienced severe food shortages. It was difficult to find enough food to feed their families, but feeding their Rottweilers could involve searching for scraps and digging through garbage cans. Fortunately, the Rottweiler is purported to have survived on these meager rations without suffering the great numbers of sterile dogs and bitches or diseased puppies that nearly devastated other German breeds at the time.

World War II

Not more than a decade after German breeders had recovered

from the severity of World War I, they would be hit with another setback. In 1939 World War II began.

As the war approached, control of dog breeding came under the Organization for German Dogs, which was run by the German Army. Regulations regarding exhibiting and breeding were passed, including a rule that for a dog to be bred, at least one of the parents had to have a Schutzhund title.

A year into World War II, in December 1940, the German Army required registration of all dogs previously approved for police work and subsequently set about testing eligible dogs for their abilities to serve in the military. The tests involved obedience, tracking, messenger, and protection work. Dogs that passed these tests were registered with the military, and approved for breeding. Owners of registered Rottweilers were given vouchers that enabled them to secure food for their dogs.

The system was a double-edged sword for breeders. Dogs that passed the tests and were registered for military service were ensured rations, but were virtually guaranteed never to return if they were called up to serve. Dogs that did not pass the test would not be called up for service, but also were not given rations, nor were they allowed to be bred.

Many of the first round of dogs approved for military service were killed, according to reports, and so the German Army increased the scope of its canine program to include more dogs approved for breeding, and a sort of buying program for puppies from approved bitches.

Post World War II

After World War II, life continued to be harsh for the German people, and subsequently for their dogs. Fortunately, through determination and sheer love of the breed, German Rottweiler breeders were able to maintain the breed. Once conditions began to improve, breeders were able to quickly bring the Rottweiler breed to the level at which it is today.

In Germany, as in many other areas of the world, the Rottweiler continues to be highly valued as a police dog. Maintaining a tremendous

Highly trainable and deeply devoted, the Rottweiler makes an excellent companion, for the right owner.

work ethic and a steadfast loyalty to his handler, the Rottweiler excels in many areas of law enforcement, including drug detection, tracking, cadaver search, and of course, apprehending suspects. Rottweilers are also used as customs dogs.

As for military service, though the German Shepherd Dog and Belgian Malinois remain the breeds of choice, Rottweilers can still be seen in the German military. In Austria, however, the Rottweiler is the dog of choice. The Austrian Army Dog School trains dogs and handlers for border patrol, guarding, and antiterrorist activities.

Other jobs the Rottweiler is frequently called upon to perform in Europe include rescue work (search and rescue), guide dogs, therapy dogs, and service dogs (for the disabled). Rottweilers can also be found in the United States performing these same functions.

Introduction to the United States

As a breed, the Rottweiler has become popular—and meteorically so—only within the last 20 years. Prior to this time, the breed was relatively obscure. In fact, the American Kennel Club (AKC) parent club for the Rottweiler, the American Rottweiler Club (ARC), was not established until 1973.

The first Rottweiler recorded in the AKC *Stud Book* appears in 1931,

with a breed standard published in 1935. The first title awarded to the breed was, appropriately, an obedience title in 1939. The first AKC championship was not awarded to a Rottweiler until 1948.

Additional national breed clubs have also formed since the inception of the ARC, and include the United States Rottweiler Club (USRC) and the American Rottweiler Verein (ARV). The USRC and ARV both sponsor Schutzhund events and European-style (FCI) conformation shows. They also offer breeding suitability tests and maintain registrations that are separate from the AKC.

Rise in Popularity

In the early 1980s the obscurity of the Rottweiler in the United States vanished. Suddenly, the great virtues of this breed were discovered and it seemed as though every American had to have a Rottweiler. By 1990 Rottweiler registrations with the AKC numbered nearly 60,500. In four years, this number jumped to 102,596. Until recently, the Rottweiler maintained the number two most popular purebred dog in registrations with the AKC.

Though the breed is popular, obviously the Rottweiler is not for everyone. Before deciding to purchase this tremendous working dog, a thorough understanding of the breed's qualities and challenges is required (see Chapter Three).

Chapter Two

The Rottweiler Today

Whether a Rottweiler fan or simply a dog enthusiast, the mere sight of a conditioned and well-bred Rottweiler commands the onlooker's attention. To see a Rottweiler perform in agility, herding, obedience or a variety of other sports is show stopping. Though the breed may look quite different today than her Roman progenitors and even her predecessors from the 1800s, the Rottweiler has developed into a striking breed that combines working abilities with brawny beauty.

The American Rottweiler Club's (ARC) breed standard reflects the club's vision of the "ideal" Rottweiler in conformation and temperament. It is by this standard that all Rottweilers in the United States are judged in the conformation ring.

Breed Standard

General Appearance

The ideal Rottweiler is a medium large, robust and powerful dog, black with clearly defined rust markings. His compact and substantial build denotes great strength, agility, and endurance. Dogs are characteristically more massive throughout with larger frame and heavier bone than bitches. Bitches are distinctly feminine, but without weakness of substance or structure.

Size, Proportion, Substance

Dogs—24 inches to 27 inches. Bitches—22 inches to 25 inches, with preferred size being midrange of each sex. Correct proportion is of primary importance, as long as size is within the standard's range.

The length of body from prosternum to the rear most projection of the rump, is slightly longer than the height of the dog at the withers, the most desirable proportion of the height to length being 9 to 10. The Rottweiler is neither coarse nor shelly. Depth of chest is approximately fifty percent of the height of the dog. His bone and muscle mass must be sufficient to balance his frame, giving a compact and very powerful appearance.

Serious faults—Lack of proportion, undersized, oversized, reversal of sex characteristics (bitchy dogs, doggy bitches).

Rottweiler, Rott, or Rottie?

What do Rottweiler breeders and owners call the breed when talking with other Rottweiler owners? Rottweiler, Rott, Rottie, or Rotten One? This is a bit of a ticklish question. In general, it is agreed that "Rottweiler" is always correct in any situation. As for the shortened forms of the name "Rottweiler," opinions vary, and be forewarned that some Rottweiler breeders and owners have *very* definite preferences. For example, one longtime respected breeder related that she and many other breeders would only abbreviate "Rottweiler" with "Rott," finding the term "Rottie" somewhat degrading. On the other hand, another breeder comments that in her circle of Rottweiler people she hears "Rott" more frequently among those with working dogs, and "Rottie" among people who deal with the breed on a daily basis and who enjoy the Rottweiler as a family companion, such as those who work at veterinary clinics and shelters, as well as police officers and pet owners.

Yet another Rottweiler owner theorized that perhaps "Rott" is the traditional abbreviation of the name, "Rottweiler," and is most common among very established breeders, whereas "Rottie" may be a name that is a more recent development and perhaps more popular among pet owners.

Interestingly, an unofficial survey conducted for the author on a popular Rottweiler e-mail list confirmed that "Rottweiler" is always correct, especially when owners are speaking with or educating the public. As for Rott or Rottie, "Rottie" was most popular among respondents, but "Rott" was also used.

So, how do you refer to the Rottweiler when talking among fellow Rottweiler owners or breeders? Well, you can't go wrong with Rottweiler. As for Rott or Rottie, be mindful that Rottweiler breeders and owners may have distinct preferences. Perhaps the best recourse is to put abbreviated Rottweiler names on the same polite conversation taboo list as politics, sex, and religion . . . . And, consider limiting the use of "Rotten One" to family and close friends!

Head

Of medium length, broad between the ears; forehead line seen in profile is moderately arched; zygomatic arch and stop well developed with strong broad upper and lower jaws. The desired ratio of backskull to muzzle is 3 to 2. Forehead is preferred dry, however some wrinkling may occur when dog is alert. *Expression* is noble, alert and self-assured. *Eyes* of medium size, almond shaped with well-fitting lids, moderately deep-set, neither protruding nor

The Rottweiler is a breed that commands attention.

Serious faults—Improper carriage (creased, folded or held away from cheek/head).

Muzzle—bridge is straight, broad at base with slight tapering towards tip, the end of the muzzle is broad with well developed chin. Nose is broad rather than round and always black. *Lips*—always black; corners closed; inner mouth pigment is preferred dark.

Serious faults—Total lack of mouth pigment (pink mouth).

Bite and Dentition—Teeth 42 in number (20 upper; 22 lower), strong, correctly placed, meeting in a scissors bite; lower incisors touching inside of upper incisors.

Serious faults—Level bite; any missing tooth.

Disqualifications—Overshot, undershot (when incisors do not touch or mesh); wry mouth; two or more missing teeth.

Neck, Topline, Body

Neck—Powerful, well muscled, moderately long, slightly arched and without loose skin.

Topline—The back is firm and level, extending in a straight line from behind the withers to the croup. The back remains horizontal to the ground while the dog is moving or standing.

Body—The chest is roomy, broad and deep, reaching to elbow, with well-pronounced forechest and well-sprung, oval ribs. Back is straight and strong. Loin is short, deep and well muscled. Croup is broad, of medium length and only slightly slop-

receding. The desired color is a uniform dark brown.

Serious faults—Yellow (bird of prey) eyes, eyes of different color, size, hairless eye rim.

Disqualification—Entropion. Ectropion.

Ears—of medium size, pendant, triangular in shape; when carried alertly the ears are level with the top of the skull and appear to broaden it. Ears are to be set well apart, hanging forward with the inner edge lying tightly against the head and terminating at approximately mid-cheek.

ing. Underline of a mature Rottweiler has a slight tuck-up. Males must have two normal testicles properly descended into the scrotum.

Disqualifications—Unilateral cryptorchid or cryptorchid males.

Tail—Tail docked short, close to body, leaving one or two tail vertebrae. The set of the tail is more important than length. Properly set, it gives an impression of elongation of topline; carried slightly above horizontal when the dog is excited or moving.

Forequarters

Shoulder blade is long and well laid back. Upper arm equal in length to shoulder blade, set so elbows are well under body. Distance from withers to elbow and elbow to ground is equal. Legs are strongly developed with straight, heavy bone, not set close together. Pasterns are strong, springy and almost perpendicular to the ground. Feet are round, compact with well arched toes, turning neither in nor out. Pads are thick and hard. Nails short, strong and black. Dewclaws may be removed.

Hindquarters

Angulation of hindquarters balances that of forequarters. Upper thigh is fairly long, very broad and well muscled. Stifle joint is well turned. Lower thigh is long, broad and powerful, with extensive muscling leading into a strong hock joint. Rear pasterns are nearly perpendicular to the ground. Viewed from the rear, hind legs are straight, strong and wide enough apart to fit with a properly built body. Feet are somewhat longer than the front feet, turning neither in nor out, equally compact with well arched toes. Pads are thick and hard. Nails short, strong, and black. Dewclaws must be removed.

Coat

Outer coat is straight, coarse, dense, of medium length and lying flat. Undercoat should be present on neck and thighs, but the amount is influenced by climatic conditions. Undercoat should not show through outer coat. The coat is shortest on head, ears and legs, longest on breaching. The Rottweiler is to be exhibited in the natural condition with no trimming.

It has been said that the Rottweiler has the uncanny capability of looking into your eyes and judging your soul.

In Germany, the Rottweiler's head is measured to assure that the proper ratio of muzzle to skull is achieved.

Fault—Wavy coat.

Serious faults—Open, excessively short, or curly coat; total lack of undercoat; any trimming that alters the length of the natural coat.

Disqualifications—Long coat.

Color

Always black with rust to mahogany markings. The demarcation between black and rust is to be clearly defined. The markings should be located as follows: a spot over each eye; on cheeks; as a strip around each side of muzzle, but not on the bridge of the nose; on throat; triangular mark on both sides of prosternum; on forelegs from carpus downward to the toes; on inside of rear legs showing down the front of the stifle and broadening out to front of rear legs from hock to toes, but not completely eliminating black from rear of pasterns; under tail; black penciling on toes. The undercoat is gray, tan, or black. Quantity and location of rust markings is important and should not exceed 10 percent of body color.

Serious faults—Straw-colored, excessive, insufficient or sooty markings; rust marking other than described above; white marking any place on dog (a few rust or white hairs do not constitute a marking).

Disqualifications—Any base color other than black; absence of all markings.

Gait

The Rottweiler is a trotter. His movement should be balanced, harmonious, sure, powerful and unhindered, with strong forereach and a powerful rear drive. The motion is effortless, efficient, and ground-covering. Front and rear legs are thrown neither in nor out, as the imprint of hind feet should touch that of forefeet. In a trot the forequarters and hindquarters are mutually coordinated while the back remains level, firm and relatively motionless. As speed increases the legs will converge under body towards a center line.

Temperament

The Rottweiler is basically a calm, confident and courageous dog with a self-assured aloofness that does not lend itself to immediate and indiscriminate friendships. A Rottweiler is self-confident and responds quietly and with a wait-and-see attitude to influences in his environment. He has

This young lady could tell you that the Rottweiler also has a soft and deeply affectionate side.

The Rottweiler's normal color is black with markings that range from rust to a deep mahogany.

an inherent desire to protect home and family, and is an intelligent dog of extreme hardness and adaptability with a strong willingness to work, making him especially suited as a companion, guardian, and general all-purpose dog.

The behavior of the Rottweiler in the show ring should be controlled, willing and adaptable, trained to submit to examination of mouth, testicles, etc. An aloof or reserved dog should be not be penalized, as this reflects the accepted character of the breed. An aggressive or belligerent attitude towards other dogs should not be faulted.

A judge shall excuse from the ring any shy Rottweiler. A dog should be judged fundamentally shy if, refusing to stand for examination, it shrinks away from the judge. A dog that, in the opinion of the judge menaces or threatens him/her, or exhibits any sign that it may not be safely approached or examined by the judge in the normal manner, shall be excused from the ring. A dog that in the opinion of the judge attacks any person in the ring shall be disqualified.

Summary

Faults—The foregoing is a description of the ideal Rottweiler. Any structural fault that detracts from the above-described working dog must be penalized to the extent of the deviation.

Disqualifications

Entropion, ectropion. Overshot, undershot (when incisors do not touch or mesh); wry mouth; two or more missing teeth. Unilateral cryptorchid or cryptorchid males. Long coat. Any base color other than black; absence of all markings. A dog that in the opinion of the judge attacks any person in the ring.

Approved May 8, 1990;
Effective June 28, 1990
Reprinted courtesy of the
American Rottweiler Club

Rottweiler Clubs

The American Rottweiler Club (ARC), is not the only national club available to Rottweiler owners. Two additional clubs also exist: The United States Rottweiler Club (USRC) and the American Rottweiler Verein (ARV). Rottweiler owners can be members of one or all of these clubs.

As the official AKC parent club for the Rottweiler, the ARC is the largest and oldest of the national Rottweiler clubs in the United States; there are several local and regional Rottweiler clubs that were founded as early as the 1950s. The ARC is also the club responsible for any decisions involving the Rottweiler breed standard. The ARC advocates well-rounded Rottweilers—those that have both beauty and brains—and encourages members to achieve both conformation and performance titles.

The USRC and ARV sanction Schutzhund events as well as European-style breeding suitability tests and conformation events. The Schutzhund titles achieved through the USRC and the ARV are not rec-ognized by the AKC, but they are recognized internationally.

For more information on the ARC, USRC, and ARV, visit their web sites, write or call for more information (see Useful Addresses and Literature, page 159).

The Rottweiler in Germany

In Germany, Rottweilers can be bred only if they have passed a stringent breeding suitability test that screens for temperament, health problems, proper conformation, and working abilities. Puppies born to one or both parents that have not passed the breeding requirements cannot be registered.

The breeding suitability test, or the Zuchttauglichkeitspröfung (ZTP), was introduced by the ADRK in the mid-1900s as a way to control the development of the breed and ensure that the original working quality of the Rottweiler is maintained. (ARV and USRC clubs sanction similar ZTP tests in the United States.) The ZTP in Germany is credited with controlling many health, temperament and conformation problems. Before a Rottweiler can be considered for the ZTP, she must first pass the entry-level title, Begleithunde (BH), or Traffic Secure Companion Dog, in Schutzhund.

The BH includes two parts: an obedience test and a temperament test. The title must be attained before a dog is allowed to achieve any additional titles in Schutzhund, including tracking (FH) and endurance (AD). The BH title is particularly important in determining that a Rottweiler has a sound and nonaggressive temperament, is safe around other dogs and people, and behaves well even with a variety of distractions, such as joggers and bicycles.

Health: German Rottweilers are required to be screened for hip dysplasia (HD) and, more recently, elbow dysplasia. One person rates all of the X-rays for the ADRK in order for there to be uniformity in the readings. The results of *all* ratings are recorded for all dogs, giving breeders a comprehensive record of all registered German Rottweilers, as well as the ability to track and spot potentially problematic lines.

Conformation: Rottweilers are examined literally from muzzle to tail and graded on everything from the color of their eyes, the proportion of muzzle length to skull, teeth placement (bite), ears, and shoulder on down to paws and most recently, the tail. Every conformation point is graded and recorded. An overall passing score with no disqualifying conformation must be achieved to pass the conformation portion of the test. Typically, owners who know their Rottweilers will not pass the conformation test, do not attempt the ZTP, so few Rottweilers taking the test fail this portion.

Performance: This portion of the ZTP involves some temperament testing and an entry level into protection work. The dog is tested for her reaction when a group of people converge on the dog and handler. The dog must show no aggression toward the people, nor may she be fearful. In another exercise, two shots are fired approximately 15 yards (14 m) from the dog and handler. The dog can show interest, but again, she cannot be fearful or aggressive.

The final portion of the performance section requires the Rottweiler to bite the protective sleeve of a "helper" in two different scenarios. These tests are really considered as a more in-depth temperament test for the dogs, since the Rottweilers must show no fear or aggression when under extreme pressure and in a stressful position. The dog must

To be a "Sieger" (champion) in Germany, a Rottweiler must also be titled in Schutzhund–an intensive sport that tests a dog's ability in obedience, tracking, and protection work.

show courage (the "bad guy" or helper acts quite menacing toward the dog) and great control; the dog must let go of the helper's arm when the helper stands still or when the handler gives the command *"Out"* (or *"Aus"* in German).

Note: "Bite work" is reminiscent of police dog training; however, in Germany many Rottweilers are being taught using the dog's play drive. What this means is that the dog is taught to bite on command, but the bite is not aggressive on the dog's part at all. Rather, the bite is a combination of the *"Take it"* and *"Hold"* commands, in which the dog is trained to take the protective sleeve that is on the helper, or "bad guy's," arm. If there's no sleeve, the dog won't bite.

The Rottweiler owner must be exceptionally conscientious in raising her dog to be both sociable and well-trained.

A dog that fails the ZTP due to a non-passing score on the protection phase may be allowed to retest at a later date. If she fails the ZTP again, the dog is declared ineligible for breeding. Dogs that pass the ZTP are granted a two-year breeding "window." They must be reevaluated at the end of this two-year period in order to be granted permanent breeding status. The ADRK additionally sets maximum age limits on breeding—nine years old for males, eight years old for females. These maximums apply even if the dog possesses permanent breeding status.

Higher Titles

At a minimum, a German Rottweiler must have passed the ZTP to be bred—but there's more. In order to be awarded the title of "Sieger," a Rottweiler must also have earned a Schutzhund title. Sieger titles are the most coveted conformation titles in Germany. There are only a handful of Sieger shows held each year in Germany, and the winning male and female are awarded Sieger (and Siegerin) titles. Males and females may win their respective classes, but they are not eligible for the German equivalent of the best of their respective sexes unless they are titled in Schutzhund. Winning in the show ring *and* achieving Schutzhund titles qualifies the German Rottweiler to achieve an even higher breeding status: Körung.

Restrictions in America

Whenever a breed surges near the top of the popularity chart, there is always talk of regulating certain aspects of the breed to maintain quality, for example, to require all dogs to be tested for hip dysplasia before being bred. This type of close regulation works in Germany, but it is important to realize that unlike the situation in the United States, the regulations in Germany are controlled by the breed club itself. In the United States, the breed club does not have the same power as it does in other countries.

The ARC has, however, enacted a mandatory ethics policy that requires member breeders to do the following:

• fully test their dogs prior to breeding
• provide contracts to puppy owners
• help place or take back their puppies or dogs that *don't* work out in homes
• carefully screen prospective owners to prevent Rottweilers from falling into the hands of disreputable owners who discredit the breed.

The ARC is also extremely active in educating the public about the Rottweiler, as well as the breed's care and training needs.

Similar efforts have been made by the USRC and ARV. They are structured much like Germany's ADRK, but participation in the USRC and ARV is strictly voluntary; therefore, control by the USRC and ARV is limited to club members. The folks who really need regulation, unfortunately, most likely don't join *any* club and therefore are not bound by any rules or codes of ethics.

Perhaps we can't control all breeding of Rottweilers, but the ARC, USRC, and ARV should be commended for the tremendous job they have done in educating the public. By showing potential Rottweiler owners what to look for in the breed and how to find reputable breeders who plan their breeding as if they were being closely regulated, these clubs are providing owners with empowering information. In addition, Rottweiler club members are held to admirable principles that reflect their true love of this breed.

Controversial Issues Facing the Breed

Every breed has some issues that are considered controversial and over which breeders and owners are often divided. As perfect as the Rottweiler is in many ways, there are some issues Rottweiler breeders and owners are being faced with, and are important for potential Rottweiler owners to be cognizant of.

Breed Bans, Dangerous-Dog Laws, and Insurance

To some extent, the saying, "There are no bad dogs, just stupid people," applies to the plight of the Rottweiler.

In recent years, often the wrong type of person has been attracted to the Rottweiler—not just in the United States, but worldwide. Drug pushers, gang members, and other disreputable people are commonly seen with Rottweilers. These owners encourage and even breed the dogs to be unsociable. The Rottweiler's inherent protective instincts are used for entirely the wrong reason and as a result, Rottweilers in the hands of disreputable owners present a highly visible, but inaccurate and dangerous representation of the breed.

Outside of the criminal element attracted to the breed, Rottweilers are also commonly popular among "macho" people who purchase a dog to toughen up their own image. Not that these folks couldn't make excellent owners, but they often have no concept about what it takes to own and care for this type of dog, which can result in an unsociable and potentially dangerous dog. Other contributors to the Rottweiler "scare" can even include the well-intentioned pet owner who purchases a Rottweiler and then has no idea how to properly raise the dog. Without the correct rearing environment, even a good Rottweiler can become dominating and develop behavior problems.

Owners, Not Breeds

A study that was performed several years ago took a close look at all fatal dog attacks during a set period. An interesting finding from the study was that the *only* consis-

tency among the non-accident bite deaths investigated was not the breed of dog, but rather that the owners of the mauling dogs were either loners or near psychopaths themselves. This discovery gives another interesting perspective into how much environment—raising the dog—affects the outcome of a dog's temperament potential.

Bites, attacks, and maulings from Rottweilers have been recorded for more than two decades. Looking at the numbers alone can be frightening, and it is not unreasonable to see why some cities have banned Rottweilers from their city limits, or why other municipalities have created dangerous-dog laws, or even why many insurance agencies have placed the Rottweiler on their blackball list of homeowner's insurance.

When the Rottweiler bites, there's a problem: While other breeds tear the skin, the Rottweiler is capable of breaking bones. But the point that excited city managers and insurance agencies are failing to look at *who* is the owner of the problem dogs. In other words, a pet owner who has purchased a well-bred Rottweiler and raised the dog in an environment that nurtures the positive behaviors of the dog, which would include responsible training, should not be punished because of dog owners who promote or foster negative behaviors.

Countering the Damage

But there are ways for responsible owners to counter the damage done by a few bad apples who are spoiling things for everyone else. In other countries, the BH title in Schutzhund is often used as proof of a dog's solid temperament. In the United States, there is a movement toward using the AKC's Canine Good Citizen (CGC) (see pages 155–156, 162) as a means to prove the dog's good temperament and perhaps as a means to qualify for homeowner's insurance with companies that have previously ousted Rottweiler owners from their list of clients.

As for city and state laws banning breeds and setting extreme dangerous-dog laws, there are several organizations working to keep abreast of these situations as they occur and help to educate the responsible lawmakers.

Inroads have been made, but as a Rottweiler owner you will have two responsibilities:

1. You must make sure that your Rottweiler is a stellar example of the breed and is well trained, sociable, and friendly. Though it may not be fair, your Rottweiler will be expected to have more tolerance and sense than humans.

2. You will need to keep a watchful eye in your community for potential onerous dog laws. For today, as one German breeder voiced, "Man does not need to fear a good Rottweiler, but a good Rottweiler has much to fear from man!"

Red Rottweilers

A hundred years ago, red coloring did exist in the breed; however, since the 1920s this color has not been accepted and is a disqualifying color. Today, there are breeders selling "red" Rottweilers. If a breeder is specifically breeding for red Rottweilers, the breeder is not ethical. Reputable breeders work to better the breed, not to introduce and perpetuate disqualifying faults, such as the red color.

Could a red Rottweiler make a good pet? Yes, if the breeder is breeding for health, temperament, and soundness. However, if the breeder is focusing on breeding for the red coloration alone, there's a high probability that temperament and health concerns have been ignored. Ultimately, the red Rottweiler is not something "special" that should command a high price tag; rather, a red Rottweiler is *strictly* a pet-quality dog that cannot be shown nor should it be bred.

Docked Tails

Rottweilers historically have had docked tails. The tail is generally docked by a veterinarian at the first or second vertebrae within just a day or two after the puppy is born. The issue over whether tails should be docked has been gaining interest not only overseas, but also in the United States. The ADRK calls for a full, natural tail for all dogs born in Germany after June 1998. Currently, the AKC breed standard for Rottweilers calls for a docked tail; however, this is expected to change in the near future. At press time for this book, the ARC was anticipated to release a tail docking shortly after birth causes little or brief pain. And finally, some Rottweiler breeders believe that docking a Rottweiler's tail will affect the dog's balance and movement adversely, since the dog has never been bred to have more than one or two vertebrae of a tail.

Proponents of the natural tail argue that tail docking at an early age is not without significant pain and stress and that cosmetic reasons alone are not a strong reason enough for a puppy's tail to be docked. Regarding the increased injuries of tailed breeds over docked breeds, those who are in favor of natural tails say the numbers of injuries are not significant, particularly when the tail is thicker, as is the Rottweiler's. As for the belief that a full tail would adversely affect the breed's movement and balance, some German breeders point out that the Rottweiler's tail acts as a rudder and actually makes for a more balanced, agile, and athletic competitor! German breeders also comment that a full tail on a Rottweiler makes the dog's intentions much easier to interpret for those inexperienced with Rottweilers—an increasingly important point for our changing society. And finally, a full tail may also enable dog-dog communication. Researchers believe that dogs with tails are better equipped to communicate with other dogs. Full-tailed dogs apparently tend to be attacked less often than dogs with docked tails, whose friendly communications may be misinterpreted.

Undocked (full-tailed) Rottweilers, such as this German puppy, are expected to be accepted by the American Rottweiler Club in the near future so that German imports can be shown in the United States without discrimination.

position statement that would recommend that Rottweilers with tails should be judged on an equal plane as those with docked tails. The concern of the club is that people would import German Rottweilers (with tails) and amputate the tail.

Proponents of the docked tail say that it gives the Rottweiler her distinctive "look." They also say that full tails are more injury prone. The argument here is that a tail injury as an adult can be very painful, whereas a

Chapter Three

The Rottweiler as a Companion

A healthy, well-groomed, obedient Rottweiler commands attention. Even when calmly lying by his master's feet, the dog exudes strength in both body and character. Without a doubt, on looks alone, the Rottweiler is an impressive, head-turning breed.

More Than Handsome

The Rottweiler is, of course, much more than a handsome dog. His true mettle goes much deeper, and as any devoted Rottweiler owner will tell you, the beauty of this breed begins with the dog's heart. Steadfast in his affections and courageous beyond bounds, the Rottweiler rightfully has earned the undying respect and loyalty of fanciers around the world.

As a powerful breed that for the past century has been bred primarily for protection, the Rottweiler possesses a complex character that must be understood and appreciated in order for the dog to become a cherished and trusted member of the family. Ironically, the same quali-

ties that draw many lifelong fanciers to the breed are those that can make the Rottweiler a bit frustrating or too challenging for even experienced dog owners.

There's no question that raising any breed of dog can be challenging—just surviving the puppy months can be an accomplishment! But the Rottweiler has certain breed characteristics that make him

The Rottweiler has a natural affinity toward children, but both child and dog must be raised to respect each other.

unique, and it is up to the potential dog owner to decide whether these characteristics are desirable or not. To put it bluntly, the Rottweiler is not a big black-and-tan cuddle toy or a preprogrammed, perfect pet. On the flip side, the Rottweiler is not an inherently vicious or aggressive dog, though thoughtless people have been known to twist them into dangerous animals. Rather, the Rottweiler is an outstanding, intelligent, athletic working dog that requires an above-average amount of training and commitment from the right kind of owner to succeed as a trusted companion dog.

Characteristics of the Rottweiler

To understand the "essence" of the multifaceted Rottweiler, it is first important to understand the varied purposes for which this dog was initially bred and translate these characteristics into modern-day situations.

Courage: As a breed required to herd cattle, the Rottweiler had to posses quick thinking, athleticism, and a level of confidence that would allow him to "stare down" or charge a full-size steer without qualms. Driving stock requires courage, wit, and stamina. The Rottweiler possesses all of these qualities, and many still make excellent herding dogs today.

Protectiveness: When working with livestock, the Rottweiler needed to be fearless in defending stock from predators, which could include wolves, bears, and other dogs. The Rottweiler also was counted on to protect his owner (the butcher) from potential thieves. Left in a solitary position, such as when he was guarding cattle for the butcher, the Rottweiler needed to be able to make his own decision about what or who posed a threat to the stock, and what or who did not. Coupled with a strong sense of territorial protectiveness, and the courage necessary to defend against a perceived "threat," the Rottweiler posed a ferocious foe to any potential predator. Today, the Rottweiler is still very protective about what he determines to be his family and his home and yard.

Quiet, calm nature: The Rottweiler is not a loud or "barky" dog, and this trait also stems from the breed's past. When working with stock, the Rottweiler needed to be relatively calm and quiet so as not to frighten the animals.

Of course, the above-mentioned characteristics of the Rottweiler are only a few aspects that draw so many pet and performance owners to the breed. Though the list of attributes of this breed is quite long, the following is a brief summary of some of the more noted strengths of this noble breed.

Activity level: As mentioned earlier, the Rottweiler is not a breed that requires constant outlets for its energy. Puppies are active, but in comparison to other breeds, they are mellow, mindful, and generally calm-natured.

Note: There are always exceptions to the rule. Some ill-bred puppies may be "hyper," nervous, or lacking in focus. This is not the classic Rottweiler temperament, but it *does* appear within the breed.

Regular, short walks will keep a puppy fit and happy, and will help with house-training. Adults are even calmer than puppies, and therefore have a more moderate activity level. A brisk morning walk or long jog in the morning and another walk in the evening is generally all that is needed to maintain a basic level of muscle tone and a healthy heart and lungs.

Adaptability: Because of the Rottweiler's relatively moderate activity level, he can fit into a variety of lifestyles and living accommodations that many other smaller but much more active breeds cannot. In other words, the adult Rottweiler may enjoy five acres of fenced property, but he can live quite well in a small home if the owner is active and committed to walking the dog several times a day to meet his exercise needs and provide the Rottweiler's necessary "outside" exploratory time.

Trainability: One of the great beauties of this breed is its willingness and ability to learn. Even as a puppy, the Rottweiler is eager to work for his owner, and readily learns and retains what he is taught. For the owner who begins his or her Rottweiler's training immediately as

Daily training that is positive and consistent is often all that is needed to establish leadership and develop a rewarding, lifelong relationship between owner and dog.

a puppy, this eagerness to please works in the owner's favor. The Rottweiler can be schooled solidly in his basic manners long before he becomes large and perhaps difficult to manage.

Constant companion: A dog should be his owner's best friend, and the Rottweiler is a breed that will make every effort to be by your side at all times. If you are an active dog owner who enjoys taking your dog everywhere you go and involving him in your everyday activities and outings, you'll find that the Rottweiler will be pleased to accompany you on all your adventures.

Affinity for children: When raised to respect and be respected by children, the Rottweiler is often described as having a particular affinity for children. Minor trespasses, such as a too tight squeeze from a young child or a tromped-on paw by a toddler, regularly go unnoticed. When the play gets too rough, the Rottweiler has the patience and presence of mind to simply rise up and walk away.

The potential Rottweiler owner should realize, however, that even though the Rottweiler seems to have a natural love of children, this characteristic is not totally inherent, and the level to which individual dogs tolerate the antics of children varies not only from dog to dog, but also with the amount of training and socialization the Rottweiler has received while growing up.

Rottweilers require daily exercise for both their mental and physical health.

All dogs, regardless of breed, should be closely supervised when with children, or separated until their interactions can be supervised. Rottweiler owners should also remember that the same amount of tolerance the dog shows the owner's own children may not be exhibited with unfamiliar children. Arguments between your child and a neighbor's child may be perceived by the Rottweiler as a threat to your child and may even elicit a protective response from the Rottweiler.

Deterrent factor: A young Rottweiler puppy won't deter anyone; in fact, the adorable puppy will *attract* a flock of people, young and old. An adult Rottweiler, however, is another matter. Dog and non-dog owners alike freely admit crossing to the other side of the street when they see a Rottweiler and his owner walking down the sidewalk. This fear is primarily unfounded and has been a source of frustration for many Rottweiler owners, particularly if the Rottweiler is well trained, socialized, and possesses the classic, calm Rottweiler temperament.

However, for the Rottweiler owner who wants to feel secure while jogging or walking in the neighborhood, the presence of a fearless, well-trained Rottweiler is in itself enough to deter most would-be rapists, thieves, and many other criminal types. If the owner adds a *bark* command with a hand signal or a verbal cue, such as, *"Watch him,"* the Rottweiler need never learn any protection training to serve his family well!

Low or no barking: When many people think of dogs that fall into the guard dog category, they often envision a growling, snarling, ferocious-sounding and -looking dog. Though extremely alert and watchful of all goings-on around the home and yard, young Rottweilers will rarely bark to alert the owner that trouble is coming. The Rottweiler usually begins voicing when he hits full maturity or around two or three years old—though he still may never bark profusely. Watchful, yes; "barky," no. (Rottweilers will, however, emit a wide range of sounds when "talking" to their owners, beginning at an early age!)

If a person is seeking an "early warning system" through a dog that barks a lot when he spots potential "trouble," the Rottweiler's silence can be disarming.

Singing and grumbling: While on the subject of barking, or rather, the Rottweiler's lack of barking, it would be remiss to not mention the interesting voicing of the Rottweiler.

• Among the most interesting voicings of the Rottweiler are his singing abilities. Throwing his head back like a wolf, the Rottweiler can break into a joyful, howling song given any number of triggers, such as other Rottweilers singing, a siren, or perhaps even the owner's own warbling.

• Another interesting sound that can emanate from a happy Rottweiler is a low mumbling, grumbling sound. Non-Rottweiler owners often panic at the first sound of this voicing because it resembles a low growling sound. Rottweiler owners, however, recognize these mumbling, grumbling sounds as an expression of sheer enjoyment from a Rottweiler that is delighting in a good tummy rub, rolling in a particularly good patch of grass, or lazing on an especially comfortable spot on the couch.

Clowning: As big and imposing as this dog can be, Rottweiler owners know, too, that their black-and-tan canine powerhouses are capable of reducing themselves to playful, wiggling clowns at any moment. Playing with balls and flipping over onto their backs to toss and hug the balls with their paws is an activity that can amuse and occupy Rottweilers for long periods of time. Generally, Rottweilers consider any excuse to play a good one, and remain playful for nearly their entire lives. Geriatric Rottweilers may refrain from too much silly play, but don't expect them to totally abstain!

Challenges in Rottweiler Ownership

As with any breed, the Rottweiler is not without its share of challenges. As mentioned previously, because of its long history as a guarding breed and its last century of work as a police, military, and protection dog, the Rottweiler may present more challenges to the average dog owner than many other more complacent and submissive breeds.

If the dog-owner relationship is to work and the Rottweiler is to become a trusted and valued member of the family—whether that's just you, or you, your spouse, kids, and grandparents—it is important to thoroughly understand the complexities of this breed and know how you will be able to meet the needs of the Rottweiler successfully.

The following are some of the challenges most often encountered in Rottweiler ownership. Not all Rottweilers will present all of these challenges, nor will all Rottweilers exhibit these traits at the same level. Each dog is unique and must be treated as such; however, this list will give you some good insight into what you might be up against and how you will need to be prepared to solve these issues.

Assertive, domineering personality: If you raise your Rottweiler from day one to respect you, your family, and your household rules, and you are consistent in enforcing these rules, your Rottweiler will most

Neutering Dominant Males

Neutering a male Rottweiler often helps to reduce the dog's desire to dominate family members and can also reduce aggression levels. If you do not plan on showing your Rottweiler, altering him can be the best option for both the dog and you (see Spay/Neuter, pages 38–40).

likely never succeed at dominating you—but this isn't to say your Rottweiler won't try. If you give your Rottweiler a toehold, he *will* try to force the issue. Rottweilers are by nature an assertive, confident breed. Males in particular will try to dominate their owners, if given the opportunity. They will look you in the eye as an equal. They will "talk" back to you when they disagree with what you've told them to do. If you've laid your groundwork well through daily training, however, and reinforce this with daily training *for the life of the dog,* the Rottweiler will be content to be "second in command."

Daily training: As mentioned above, daily training is necessary for the success of the Rottweiler to reinforce who is in command and who is next in command. This is not a breed that can be taught the basic commands as a puppy and be expected to respect these commands for a lifetime. Daily training, however, does not mean that an owner has to spend an hour each evening with his dog performing complicated and demanding obedience exercises. It *does* mean that within each day, the owner dedicates 10 to 20 minutes to reviewing basic commands and requiring the Rottweiler to perform these commands with some precision. Just this little bit of time spent each day will help to keep order in the household.

By the way, all members of the family, grandparents that visit frequently, baby-sitters and nannies should all be involved at some level in the Rottweiler's training. He must learn to respect all members of the extended family, and the best way to do this is to have everyone reinforcing the dog's training under the supervision of the "lead" trainer in the family.

Territoriality: One of the reasons the Rottweiler has skyrocketed in popularity over the past 10 to 15 years is that many owners are seeking a dog that will protect their home and family and provide a sense of safety. Unfortunately, to buy a dog strictly for protection purposes is entirely the wrong reason. Many of the people who purchase a Rottweiler with the explicit purpose of guarding a home quickly find out that the level of effort and expertise needed to train and maintain a protection dog is intense and time consuming; a security alarm system linked to a protection service would be much simpler.

Those who purchase the Rottweiler not realizing that this breed is very protective of his property and people are also in for a big surprise. The Rottweiler is very territorial. This is part of the essence of the Rottweiler. To the pet owner, this means that he or she will need to work regularly with the Rottweiler to keep the dog's territorial aggressiveness in control. A dog that is ultrapossessive of his owner and/or home, and that is not very well trained will someday hurt someone or something.

Rottweiler owners must be willing to take the time to properly socialize and train their dogs to be model

Rottweilers like to be where you are, no matter what you are doing.

canine citizens, and not purposefully or indirectly encourage their dogs to be dangerously protective of their yards and homes. This takes time, effort, and diligence. The rewards of these efforts are many, but it is a serious commitment on the part of the owner.

Shadowing: One of the joys of owning a Rottweiler is that of having a constant companion, always in sight, and usually right at your feet or with his head in your lap. The Rottweiler enjoys being close to his family. A dog that is denied this privilege—one that is banished to a room or to the backyard—can become destructive and even aggressive.

When in the home and allowed to be a member of the family, sometimes the Rottweiler's physically demonstrative affection may be too much for some owners. If a constant shadow or canine "presence" is *not* the type of dog you had in mind, the Rottweiler may *not* be the unobtrusive dog you are searching for. This is a dog that wants, needs, and thrives with attention. This does not mean you have to allow a 120-pound (54 kg) Rottweiler to be a lapdog (ouch!). It just means that you should be prepared to dole out the pats and ear scratches, and allow your treasured companion to be able to watch you and follow you around the house. Remember: The Rottweiler is your self-appointed guardian. Allowing him to do his "job" will give him immense pleasure.

Shedding: Though the Rottweiler's black-and-tan coat looks as if it would require minimal care, it is not as carefree as a shorthaired breed. The Rottweiler's double coat has a course, outer hair and a softer, warm undercoat. The breed typically sheds profusely in spring and fall, and loses hair on a regular basis at all other times of the year. The Rottweiler needs to be brushed regularly whether he is during shedding season or not. And even with this attention, there can still be a bit of hair floating around the house. If the occasional wafting hair clump is unacceptable in your home, you will need to be extra vigilant in your grooming or consider a curly or tightly coated breed that does not drop hairs as easily.

Drooling: The Rottweiler doesn't drool any more than other breeds with the same relative mouth and lip formation; however, if you're used to owning a "tight-lipped" breed that never drools, the Rottweiler may be a bit more than you're used to. He will drool when excited, when anticipating food, and during and after exercise. A good head shaking after a period of drooling can fling things around a bit, but nothing that a swipe with a towel can't take care of.

Chewing: Rottweilers are *big* chewers. With an approximate bite pressure of 25 pounds per inch (11 kg per 2.5 cm), the Rottweiler can quickly destroy all but the sturdiest of chew toys. And, don't think chewing is just a puppy phase with these guys—even after all their adult teeth are in, Rottweilers love to chew. Be prepared to keep your Rottweiler supplied with lots of safe, indestructible, hard rubber, stuffable toys and large, sturdy bones.

The foot thing: Rottweilers have a sort of reverse foot fetish—they *don't* like to have their feet handled. Handling the Rottweiler's feet on a daily basis from the time he is a tiny puppy helps, but does not totally solve the problem. If you want to be able to clip your Rott's toenails without muzzling him or taking him to the pet groomer, you will need to be diligent in working with your dog's paws and nails to overcome or lessen this "foot thing," (see information on care of eyes, ears, nails, and teeth in Chapter Ten).

Rott'n gas: Let's just say that it pays to be very careful what you feed your Rottweiler. Excessive treats, foods high in soy or soy products, and "people" food can cause your Rottweiler to emit rather fragrant fumes. (For more information on what to feed your Rottweiler, see Nutrition, page 106.)

Exercise needs: Even though your Rottweiler has a moderate activity level, he still needs to be exercised daily. The reason for this is twofold. One is that a basic level of exercise is needed to maintain your Rottweiler's health. Two is that a walk around the neighborhood allows your Rottweiler a chance to see the outside world, helps to lessen his inherent territorial feeling, and continues to socialize your Rottweiler with all sorts of people.

Fence and leash precautions: For the safety of your Rottweiler and for others, your Rottweiler must never be able to run off leash at any time. This means that the Rottweiler owner must invest in a sturdy, tall fence for the backyard. A Rottweiler on a chain in an open yard is not acceptable and can encourage aggressive behavior. The Rottweiler should not be allowed to run loose in an unfenced area or walked off leash, either. The owner must *always* walk the Rottweiler on a leash and be in control of the dog at all times. Because of the power and strength of the Rottweiler, this is not a dog that children should be allowed to walk without supervision.

Health disorders: The Rottweiler is predisposed to several diseases, some of which can be life-threatening (see Common Diseases of the Rottweiler, Chapter Twelve). The potential Rottweiler owner should be aware of these diseases and should be willing to take the time necessary to find a reputable breeder who screens for these hereditary diseases and provides a written health guarantee.

Legal and moral responsibilities: Because the Rottweiler is a protection breed, and because it has received a lot of publicity in recent years—most of which has been bad—Rottweiler ownership carries with it additional legal and moral responsibilities than are found with few other breeds of dogs. In some areas of the country, breed-specific laws make Rottweiler ownership illegal. And, across the country, insurance agencies are denying homeowner's insurance to Rottweiler owners (see Breed Bans, Dangerous-Dog Laws, and Insurance," page 19).

In addition to these troublesome woes, the Rottweiler owner is faced with the stark reality that yes, indeed, a bite from a Rottweiler is a serious injury. With the Rottweiler's incredible jaw pressure (a single bite from a Rottweiler can break bones; whereas, another dog's bite may barely break the skin), the breed carries with it a tremendous liability. One inopportune bite can spell euthanasia for the Rottweiler, and a major lawsuit for the owner, not to mention a very injured person or pet.

As one animal behaviorist pointed out, owning a Rottweiler is similar to owning the biggest, most expensive, sport utility vehicle on the market. In itself, the SUV is not a dangerous vehicle. When mishandled, however, it can be a lethal weapon. And even when it is in good hands, it can

Perhaps the greatest danger of owning a Rottweiler is that an enthusiastic dog can accidentally topple young children and frail adults.

become involved in an accident. When in an accident, the larger vehicle inherently causes much more damage than the smaller car, and the damages can be costly and difficult to fix. This is a good point and one all potential Rottweiler owners should consider. The Rottweiler is one of the most loyal and courageous of all dog breeds, but these qualities come with a need for the owner to be responsible and committed to the training and care of his or her dog.

Big Dog Ownership

Along with the challenges of owning a Rottweiler, there are also challenges linked simply with owning any big dog. If you've never owned a dog this size before, be sure to consider what it's like to own a dog that

routinely tips the scales at 100+ pounds (45+ kg).

Clean counters: Nothing is safe on the counters any longer when you own a Rottweiler. If the Rottweiler can't see it, he can smell it, and access to the counter is just a tiptoe away. Meat, vegetables, bread—it doesn't matter. It's gone. Big dog owners quickly learn to crate their dogs when they can't watch them, or keep all food stuffs out of reach and behind closed doors. Rottweilers have been known to learn how to open refrigerator doors, so some additional owner ingenuity—or a set of bungee cords—may be necessary!

Bowling over children, frail adults: It's true that Rottweilers sometimes don't realize their size. Though generally gentle with children, they can become excited and accidently knock over a child. Frail or unsteady adults also can be tumbled by a bump from a well-meaning Rottweiler. If an occasional bowling over is unacceptable in your home, you will need to closely supervise your Rottweiler's activities, or perhaps consider a smaller, less physical dog.

Higher food bills: Big dogs do eat more than very small dogs, so your food bills will be appreciably higher than that of, say a toy or small breed. Along with the healthy appetite also comes bigger clean-up chores. Keep this in mind as you look at your neatly manicured yard.

Expenses: Large-breed dogs can cost more than their smaller counterparts:

1. Large crates cost more than small crates.

2. Neutering/spaying costs more with a large breed than with a small breed.

3. Some medications, such as heartworm preventive are calculated by weight, and—you guessed it—larger doses cost more. If money is tight, you may want to wait to purchase a Rottweiler until you can save up some funds.

Rental considerations: Few rental properties approve dogs that weigh more than 20 pounds (9 kg)—and don't think you can sneak a full-grown Rottweiler into your apartment without anyone noticing! Even if you can convince the manager or property owner to allow you to keep a Rottweiler on the rental property, you may be required to pay a full month's rent as a deposit against potential damages. Additionally, the property owner—because this is a Rottweiler—may require you to take out costly insurance to cover any potential incidents with other dogs or even people.

If you are a renter, or if renting is a possibility in the future, be sure to select a Rottweiler as your dog only *if* you are committed to searching until you find a home to which you can take your Rottweiler with you. Large-dog owners have been known to purchase homes because they could not find rental properties that would accept their large dogs. Are you this committed? The Rottweiler will give you his life; make sure you are committed to taking care of this precious gift for his entire lifetime, however long that might be.

Do You Have What It Takes?

You don't have to be a weight lifter to be able to handle a Rottweiler. In fact, the physical strength of the owner should never be an issue. A petite, 5'2" (157 cm) woman weighing a mere 100 pounds (45 kg) can handle a Rottweiler that easily outweighs her by 20 pounds (9 kg) or more—if she has the right leadership skills and understands and can skillfully deal with the complexities of her Rottweiler's character.

Leadership

The biggest key to Rottweiler ownership is for the Rottweiler owner to be every bit as confident and unintimidated with the Rottweiler as the Rottweiler is with the owner. Dog owners who are fearful of a fully grown Rottweiler will find the Rottweiler immediately taking advantage of the situation and doing whatever he wants, whenever he wants. If, within a household, a spouse or child is fearful or intimidated by the dog, this is the person the dog will begin to dominate first. If left unchecked, a few bumps and stares from the dog can become growls, snarls, and even bites. Without firm, but kind, leadership from all household members, the Rottweiler will try to force the issue.

Toehold: A successful Rottweiler owner, in addition to being self-confident, will never allow the dog to get away with even what seems to be minor indiscretions, such as not moving off the couch when you want to sit down. With another breed, when a dog doesn't want to move, it could simply mean that the dog is tired and lazy. With the Rottweiler, it could be a subtle attempt (the toehold) to test who's in charge and who gets out of whose way. If you tell the dog to move and he doesn't, and you sit in another chair, consider this "Rottweiler: 1, Owner: 0." And, the Rottweiler never forgets . . . Once the dog is allowed to get away with dominant behaviors, his efforts to gain even more control may elevate to bumping, threatening stares, a low rumble, or even a snarl, snap, or bite.

Physical Corrections: The assertive owner, like an admired school teacher, is gentle but firm and is able to command respect *without* physical corrections. Leadership qualities do not come naturally to all people; however, many people are quiet, but strong leaders, and do not realize their full capabilities. If you are not sure if you have what it takes to be successful with a Rottweiler, make sure to take some time to visit with and talk to reputable Rottweiler breeders, owners, and trainers. Watch how they work with their dogs, how they interact, and judge for yourself whether you feel comfortable in the commander's role or not.

If you are not entirely comfortable with your leadership abilities, you may want to consider a breed that shows more submissiveness. (Few Rottweilers are submissive.) Or, you may want to consider working with a reputable Rottweiler rescue organization to help you find an adult or near-adult Rottweiler that is a known entity and will mesh well with your handling abilities (see Adopting the Adult Rottweiler, pages 60–69).

Lifestyle

Another consideration to make when thinking about becoming a Rottweiler owner, is whether you have a lifestyle that is favorable for dog ownership. If you want to raise a Rottweiler puppy, but you are single and work long hours or your family is overloaded with work, after school sports, or other activities, this may not be the best time in your life to attempt this endeavor. Puppy raising can be intense (see the discussion of Benefits and drawbacks of puppy ownership in Chapter Four), and requires that someone is available to provide care for the young puppy every few hours during the day and can take the time to train the Rottweiler.

That's not to say that a busy owner or family can't make things work. With a little creativity, ingenuity, and the flexibility to make lifestyle changes to adapt to the Rottweiler's needs, a puppy or adopted dog can be raised successfully in virtually any household. The important thing is to recognize exactly what the puppy or adult Rottweiler's needs are, and come up with solutions that will work for you and the Rottweiler.

Chapter Four

The Rottweiler's Life Stages

As a breed, Rottweilers take a little longer to mature than many smaller dogs. A Rottweiler will nearly reach her full height by the age of 12 months, but she won't fill out for another one to two years. From the moment she is born, however, the Rottweiler will go through many important physical, mental, and emotional milestones that will influence how she presents herself as an adult. It is particularly important for the Rottweiler owner to understand these various phases of development in order to provide the correct learning experiences that will help to mold an enjoyable, socially responsible adult dog.

Prenatal

From the moment of conception, forces are beginning to take effect that will influence the development of your future Rottweiler. During the two months that it takes for the Rottweiler to transform from a tiny embryo to a fully developed fetus, researchers have found that the health and emotional state of the mother are very important.

We already know that genetics play a strong role in the predisposed temperament of the puppies, but what this new research tells us is that *imprinting* occurs *before the puppies are even born.* For example, in one study researchers showed that if a female is given loving attention, and stroked and petted during her gestation period, the attention and physical handling affects her unborn puppies' tolerance to being stroked and touched later. A breeder, therefore, who treats his or her dogs with compassion and care is facilitating the future temperaments of the puppies. Alternatively, studies indicate that a stressful mother, such as one that is kept in isolation in a cage under appalling conditions, will transmit her feeble physical and emotional health to some degree to her puppies.

Poor health is another prenatal factor that can be passed along to unborn puppies. An underfed, malnourished mother is not going to have the essential nutrients to provide her growing puppies—during gestation or after whelping. Dogs that are not fully screened by a veterinarian prior to breeding may have diseases or conditions that could adversely affect the health of the puppies. Hereditary diseases are certainly passed along to the puppy before it is ever born.

In other words, how well a female is cared for before, during, and after whelping are critical elements affecting the well-being of the puppies. Yet another reason to choose a knowledgeable, experienced, and caring breeder!

Neonatal

Newborn puppies are born with their eyes closed, weigh little more than a pound, and are entirely dependent on their mother. The newborn puppies react to the smell of their mother's milk and automatically know how to suckle. They can

Between the ages of two and sixteen weeks, the Rottweiler puppy will go through a critical period for learning the appropriate social attitude toward other dogs and people.

also cry, whimper, and growl, but their mobility is limited to dragging themselves around. Later, when they gain more control, they will begin to walk and trot. Well-fed puppies that are in good health can expect to double their weight within eight to nine days.

In the first few days of a Rottweiler's life, milk teeth appear. These teeth will stay with the puppy until she is about four or five months old. Within the first few days, if a Rottweiler is to have her tail "docked," the procedure is performed by a veterinarian. The tails are usually cut very closely, leaving only one or two vertebrae. At this time, the puppies will also have dewclaws removed from the rear legs, if they are present, and from the forelegs, if the breeder chooses to have this optional procedure performed.

The Young Puppy: Two to Sixteen Weeks

By the age of two weeks, the Rottweiler puppies will have their eyes open and will begin to see quite well within the next few days. During their early months, the puppies go through some critical phases in learning that begin to mold their attitudes toward people and other dogs.

Socialization with People

As a tiny puppy, the Rottweiler begins to learn about humans. For this reason, breeders try to handle the puppies frequently and make sure that their experiences with people are positive and fun. Often, breeders will have children come over to play with the puppies so that the pups grow up enjoying this interaction. In this way, the Rottweiler puppies become familiar with the unique sounds, motions, and noises of children.

At eight weeks, when many puppy owners will be picking up their puppies, the puppy's socialization with people continues. Puppies must be introduced to all sorts of people, of all size, races, and ages, from little toddlers to senior citizens, from postal workers in uniforms to the neighbor who wears a baseball cap. These introductions must be kept positive and friendly, and the puppy should always be rewarded for behaving nicely when she meets and greets new people (see Socialization, page 47). This training should continue through the life of the dog to reinforce good socialization skills.

Contact with Other Dogs

While the puppy is with her mother and littermates, she is learning valuable lessons about how to act and behave with other puppies. She learns that if she plays too roughly or makes another puppy scream, that puppy won't want to play with her. She also learns from her mother how to behave around adult dogs. Living with littermates and having continued contact with the mother has been

A Rottweiler that was well socialized as a puppy should easily accept other dogs as an adult.

indicated by some studies to promote bite inhibition.

Studies have also shown that if a puppy is removed from her littermates before she is seven weeks old, which often occurs with puppy mill products and with inexperienced breeders, the puppy will suffer mentally from this early separation. Problems that might ensue include a lack of submission as a puppy to adult dogs, and later, abnormal behavior as an adult. Even with skilled training and behavioral intervention, some of these behaviors cannot be corrected. Therefore, though purchasing a puppy at six weeks may seem tempting, it is not a good idea. Wait, and purchase the puppy that is available at eight weeks or older.

Once you bring your puppy home, it is important to keep positive contact between the young puppy and other dogs. The difficulty lies in the fact that the puppy is not resistant to many diseases at this time, so playmates must be *very* carefully selected. Introductions to other dogs also need to be a positive experience. The puppy that is attacked or bitten by an adult dog will remember this and may be more prone to grow aggressive toward other dogs.

The Middle-aged Puppy: Four to Eight Months

This is a period of rapid growth and a time of good experiences and challenges. You can expect your Rottweiler to be gaining strength, coordination, and weight rapidly during this time period. You don't want your Rottweiler to become fat as a developing puppy, however, because extra weight will put an undue strain on her growing bones and joints, which could cause temporary discomfort or even permanent damage.

Control

Perhaps one of the most exciting prospects during this developmental period is that your Rottweiler puppy will be gaining more control of her bodily functions. She might already have a good grasp on managing to control defecation, but now she will begin to show better control of her bladder. She should be able to

"hold" for up to eight hours during nonactive times, as while sleeping, and possibly up to five hours during the day—after having been walked, of course.

Teething

With the gain in control comes a dreaded phase of puppyhood: teething. Between four and five months of age, the Rottweiler puppy will lose her milk teeth and adult teeth will begin erupting. Teething can be a miserable time for both the puppy that is experiencing discomfort, itching gums, and perhaps even pain from the new teeth. It is also a difficult time for the owner, who is frantically trying to keep up with his or her pup's voracious appetite for chewing *everything* and *anything*.

To get through this phase, make sure to have plenty of safe toys and chews available at all times for the puppy (see Toys, Toys, Toys, page 75 for some ideas on what is safe and what is not.) Be sure to rotate the toys and chews so that your puppy doesn't become bored with the same items every day. One way to do this is to have an assortment of up to twelve items and rotate which eight items you have out for your puppy each day.

Spay/Neuter

If you don't plan on showing your Rottweiler or competing in performance events, then any time around six months is a good time to consider spaying or neutering your Rottweiler. The surgery is also sometimes performed as early as

Tug-of-War

In the Rottweiler community, and among trainers, veterinarians, and animal behaviorists there are some very different opinions over whether or not a Rottweiler owner—or *any* dog owner—should play tug-of-war with a dog. The controversy is over whether playing tug causes a dog to become more dominant. The consensus is that if the dog is always allowed to win the game, then yes, this could cause a dog to believe he was higher ranking in status than the rest of the family, particularly the individual she beats in the game.

Trainers say you can alleviate this problem with most dogs by teaching the dog that she must quit playing and release the tug toy to the owner *on command.* This means that before the game of tug is ever introduced, even with a young puppy, the Rottweiler must sit when the owner directs her to, and then *out* or release the tug toy into the owner's hand. The Rottweiler should be allowed to win the game to build self-confidence (what's the fun in *always* losing?), but the exercise of requiring an *out* command from time to time should be enough to satisfy both your need for leadership and your dog's needs for having fun.

Is tug a game you should play with your Rottweiler? It probably depends. If you are already having problems with dominance and getting your Rottweiler to heed commands, then absolutely not; you're setting your Rottweiler up to fail. If you have a dog that is very good with her commands and has shown no attempts to change the leadership, can you play tug? It should be no problem if you remember to require an *out* from time to time and at the end of play.

One additional thought: Some Rottweiler breeders advise never to play tug with a young or growing Rottweiler puppies because it could put undue stress on their hips.

eight weeks—and you may find that you are purchasing a puppy from a breeder that has already altered his or her puppies. There are many advantages to having a dog spayed or neutered, and not the least of them is that it improves the health of your dog by preventing certain cancers. There are, of course, other reasons to perform this surgery.

Males: An intact male can be a difficult dog to handle. When the hormones start surging and the scent of an available female is carried to your Rottweiler's discerning nose, you've got trouble on your hands. Your formerly well-trained, obedient male Rottweiler may try to do anything and everything to escape his home and yard to find

Neutering can help control some of the potential difficulties normally associated with owning an intact male.

And finally, if your male is neutered, his risk of ever suffering from testicular cancer is nil. (If you'd like your dog to "appear" to be intact, you can have implants inserted that are designed precisely for this reason.)

Females: Unspayed females have their challenges, as well. When in season, a female Rottweiler may dig, jump, and bolt out the door in search of males. She will attract canine suitors from literally miles away. If you have intact males in your home, you must ensure that they are kept separate from your female. You may also have to keep the males separated from each other, as a female in season can spawn terrible fights between the males. A female in season also has a difficult time keeping herself clean, and may need to be crated or kept in an area in which you can clean up after her.

Spaying a Rottweiler will prevent your female from coming into season. It will also prevent uterine cancer as well as other female reproductive diseases. The risk of mammary cancer may be reduced by the spaying, too, if performed before the female's first or second heat cycle.

that female. This includes bolting out of doors, digging under fences, and climbing out of the backyard. He may also become irritable with other family pets, particularly other dogs that he might see as challenging his ability to get to that female.

An intact male is certainly more interested in reproducing than an altered male, but he may also be more aggressive toward other dogs and perhaps even people. Some studies indicate that when an aggressive dog is neutered, as many as 60 percent see substantial, positive changes in their behaviors.

The Adolescent Rottweiler

The adolescent Rottweiler is nearly full height, but as mentioned previously, it will be some time before she fills out and possesses the muscular physique of an adult. However, as with a human adolescent, the adolescent Rottweiler thinks she's an adult *now* and may try to assert her authority—both with you and with other dogs.

Challenges to People

As discussed in Chapter Three, the Rottweiler is a self-confident, non-submissive dog. This translates to a Rottweiler that is a willing worker under an accepted leader; however, if at any time she thinks there is an opportunity to begin to work into the leadership role, she might take it. Acutally, this quality holds equally true for males and females.

A dog that has been in training since the time she was a puppy generally presents no problems to the owner if the owner continues to require his or her Rottweiler to "work" every day. The owner who doesn't make his or her Rottweiler work for treats and praise and who allows minor transgressions from the Rottweiler, such as allowing the Rottweiler to get up on a chair that is supposed to be forbidden, may quickly see himself or herself getting into trouble.

Rottweilers don't forget, which compounds the problem. If you allow her to get away with something one time, she won't forget this and will challenge you the next time you ask her to obey. How you handle this challenge, which could be a Rottweiler glare, lying down and refusing to budge, or even a discontented grumbling, will affect how your Rottweiler responds the next time you ask her to obey. In other words, one slip on your part—even if in kindness—will require more time to undo the damage. Simply said, set your Rottweiler up for success by not allowing any transgressions and reinforcing the leadership role through regular, daily training.

Challenges to Other Pets

Usually, when left to their own devices, dogs will establish a general pecking order within a household. This pecking order is typically maintained in harmony until the leader—usually the oldest dog—begins to fail in health or dies. Dog owners who have had dogs coexist in a pack for years report that the death of the lead dog can cause the remaining dogs to quickly deteriorate into a squabbling pack.

A rising young male or female can also toss this pack harmony into jeopardy. For example, if a young male Rottweiler is raised with an older Cocker Spaniel, the two may grow up to live in relative peace, if the Cocker Spaniel is not a dominant dog and is willing to accept that the Rottweiler is bigger and better at leading than he is. If the older dog does not want to relinquish his command, an intact, adolescent Rottweiler may try to force the issue. At the very least, the adolescent Rottweiler will not tolerate being bullied—and he won't forget if the older dog bullied him while he was a puppy either.

Though many female Rottweilers live together in relative peace, a rising, adolescent female can also be a problem and may try to challenge the leader of the females. Females can get in horrible fights and may not stop fighting unless permanently separated, or until one of the females dies. A female Rottweiler living with a female of another breed of dog may not have any problems, if the other dog is submissive. Generally, female Rottweilers will live with a male Rottweiler or other dog without a problem, and vice versa.

To sum up, if you have other dogs in the family, it is wise to carefully supervise their interactions and keep an eye out for any potential problems. Neutering can certainly change the climate among males; females may be more complex in working out their relationships. Though Rottweilers can and do get along in pairs and packs, the pairing with the best chance of success is, of course, a neutered male with a spayed female. Other successful pairings can be a Rottweiler with a submissive, altered dog of another breed.

All Grown Up

Once your Rottweiler is mature, her activity level should be less than that of an adolescent, and in some instances may regress to the point of her becoming a couch potato. If you have a Rottweiler that is prone to melt into the softest piece of furniture available, you might need to encourage regular exercise. If your Rottweiler has gotten out of shape, remember to start slowly and build up to longer distances. The Rottweiler is a working dog and will be happiest if she is kept in good shape and can accompany you on your walks or runs.

As your Rottweiler reaches maturity and continues into adulthood, you should maintain a vigilant eye for certain diseases, such as cancer, that could develop in the middle-aged adult. For a complete listing of potential health problems that can develop in the adult Rottweiler, see Chapter Twelve: Common Diseases of the Rottweiler.

Also, even though your Rottweiler has received training while she was a growing puppy, she should continue to be schooled in good man-

You'll only be able to pick up your Rottweiler for a very short while!

ners every day, and should continue to work for treats. As was covered earlier in this chapter, this continued gentle and positive training is generally all that is needed to maintain a good leadership position with your Rottweiler.

Senior Citizens

As your Rottweiler ages, she may require extra care. Older Rottweilers may need to be encouraged to get out and exercise. They may require a modification in their feeding—less food or lower calories—to accommodate their slowing metabolism. The senior's diet may need to be more highly palatable, too, because as dogs age, they are thought to lose some of their sense of taste, much in the same way as aging humans do. Additionally, geriatric dogs may not be able to assimilate food as well as they did as youngsters, so it becomes increasingly important that their food is highly digestible in order for the senior to get all her necessary nutrients.

Some diseases can cause the aging Rottweiler considerable pain. Arthritis and hip dysplasia are two such diseases that can become crippling for a large dog. If your senior is showing signs of discomfort, she should be taken to the veterinarian for a complete exam. There are many things that can be done to aid in reducing the discomfort experienced from aches, pains, and swelling.

Incontinence: Older dogs may also suffer from incontinence. If your Rottweiler, who has been perfect in house-training all her life, suddenly begins having accidents, consult your veterinarian. There are some medications available to help with incontinence. Additionally, the dog may be incontinent because she is suffering from an illness, such as a bladder infection, that can be treated by your veterinarian.

Even if the incontinence cannot be treated with medications, depending on the severity of the situation, there are many products available to help with incontinent dogs, ranging from special pads that wick moisture away from the dog to beds that are constructed with a mesh floor to allow liquids to drain. Sometimes simply returning to a strict eating, drinking, and walking (relieving) schedule can be enough to assist your dog and alleviate accidents. Dog doors from a room in the house to the fenced backyard can be another helpful option for your dog, allowing her to relieve herself whenever she needs to.

How Far to Go and Letting Go

It used to be that the most heartbreaking decision involved with dog ownership was in making the final decision to euthanize a dog to relieve her from a painful, terminal illness. With our age of increased

This 12-year-old dog is enjoying his senior years because his owner has taken great care to provide for all his needs throughout his life.

technology and treatment options, however, there is a more agonizing question for owners that is arising: "How far should I go?"

This is where the most heart-wrenching decision making comes in: choosing whether to treat a dog's symptoms for hip dysplasia with medications, or to have the full-blown hip surgery performed; deciding whether to euthanize a dog suffering from terminal cancer when the pain becomes too great, or opting for aggressive costly treatments without a cure, but only a hope that they will extend the dog's life a short while.

The best advice is to set aside your personal feelings and listen to your veterinarian's advice, get second or third opinions if you're unsure. And, most important, listen to your Rottweiler. You must balance the prognosis for your Rottweiler with her comfort and, of course, with your physical and financial abilities.

No one knows for sure how long our Rottweilers will live. All we can really do is provide the best possible care and cherish these magnificent dogs while they are with us. Hopefully, your Rottweiler will live a full and healthy life, but it is best never to take anything for granted.

Chapter Five

Choosing the Rottweiler Puppy

If puppies were judged on a scale of cuteness from 1 to 10, Rottweiler puppies would surely score an 11. Few people can resist playing with a healthy, bouncy, furry black-and-mahogany bundle that exudes pure puppy love. Without question, Rottweiler puppies are among the most attractive of puppies and their inquisitiveness, intelligence, and sheer joy of life never fails to entrance potential puppy owners.

What Puppy Ownership Involves

Puppy ownership, particularly with a Rottweiler, is not all fun and games. It involves a lot of hard work, sleepless nights, and a good dose of patience to make it through the puppy's first year. That's not to say that raising a puppy from the time he is only a couple of months old doesn't have tremendous benefits. It's just that sometimes the responsibilities involved in raising a Rottweiler puppy can be overwhelming for some owners—particularly those who don't know what they're getting into.

For this reason alone it is wise for a potential puppy owner to understand exactly what is involved in raising a Rottweiler. Armed with this knowledge, a puppy owner can avoid rearing mistakes that might affect the dog's temperament, health, or behavior. On the other hand, the potential Rottweiler owner, with a knowledge of just what raising a Rottweiler entails, may choose instead to adopt a rescued Rottweiler and avoid many of the problems of puppyhood (see Adopting the Adult Rottweiler, pages 60–69).

The following are some key points—both good and challenging—that are necessary to know when raising a Rottweiler.

Benefits of Puppy Ownership

Obviously, one of the advantages to owning a Rottweiler puppy is that they are absolutely adorable. This is a once-in-a-lifetime phase, and when a Rottweiler is grown up, he may still be very playful but he won't ever be that little bundle of black-and-rust fur again. However, there are many other reasons to choose a Rottweiler as a puppy. Following are

Don't be fooled: This little guy can wreak havoc–all in the name of fun, of course.

some of the areas in which you can influence the growth of your Rottweiler puppy:

Temperament: Researchers believe that as much as 40 percent of a dog's temperament is a result of the dog's environment and experiences while growing up. This means that as an owner, you have an incredibly profound impact on the temperament of your Rottweiler. If you raise your Rottweiler puppy to be a good-natured, congenial dog, the odds are in your favor that your dog will develop into a tremendous companion.

Good health: It is correct that you can't *change* the inherited health (genetic diseases) of a puppy; however, if you raise a Rottweiler as a puppy, there is much you can do to foster good health and prevent illnesses. Quality food, fresh water, exercise, and regular, excellent veterinary care will do much to help develop the vigor of your growing Rottweiler. A full series of vaccinations will prevent many life-threatening disease and regular heartworm preventive will ward off this deadly parasite (see Preventive Care, page 112). It is even believed that gentle exercise, good diet, and maintaining a proper weight can do much to prevent or lessen the onset of certain bone and joint disorders.

Acclimating to lifestyle: Though there are adult dogs that can walk into a new home and settle in within days, it is generally much easier for a dog to adapt to a household as a puppy. As a young dog, puppies are very malleable. They see new sounds and sights and generally adapt to them readily—if introduced to them in a positive way.

Respect: Another benefit of raising a Rottweiler as a puppy is that during the development of the Rottweiler, the puppy can be taught to respect all members of the family, from the smallest toddler to a live-in grandparent. The puppy can be taught from day one to be handled and respond to commands from all family members regardless of size or strength, preventing potential future issues over leadership.

Ease in training: Training a puppy that is small, willing, and eager to learn is much simpler than teaching a large, unruly animal that isn't sure he needs to obey you.

Pitfalls of Puppyhood

Rottweiler puppies are cute, impressionable, and easily trained as youngsters, but it wouldn't be fair to say this breed isn't without its challenges as a puppy. Some of the most common problems involving Rottweiler puppies are listed below.

Activity level: The Rottweiler is known as a relatively calm dog with a moderate activity level. A mature Rottweiler likes to have fun, but he does not have the high activity levels of some of the on-the-go sporting breeds and nonstop terriers. However, what many owners fail to recognize is that the Rottweiler puppy is a puppy, and puppies naturally have higher activity levels. So, if you can't tolerate high bursts of energy for up to two years from a growing, large puppy (that sometimes has coordination and sometimes doesn't), then you may want to consider adopting an adult dog that already has the calm demeanor you are looking for.

Teething: This is generally a very trying time for puppy owners and requires a lot of patience, and consistency in training. Because of the Rottweiler's incredible jaw strength, this chewing phase can be quite destructive and, depending on what items your Rottweiler seeks out to chew, this phase can also be quite expensive.

Obedience: With a Rottweiler puppy, there is no exception to the training rule. All Rottweiler puppies need to begin training as soon as possible, and this training must continue through their lives. But training takes time, effort, and patience—things a potential dog owner may not always have.

Socialization: Socialization is important for all puppies, but with the Rottweiler, it is *critical*. Because of the breed's reputation as being potentially dangerous, and the breed's natural instincts to be protective, the puppy owner *must* devote a significant amount of time during the puppy's first year to socialize him with people of all kinds and other dogs (see The Rottweiler's Life Stages, pages 35–44). Since the key period for socialization begins the moment you bring your puppy home, this is not an activity that can

How you raise your puppy can have a profound influence on her health and temperament, so be sure you are ready to accept this responsibility.

be picked up later; it must be accomplished at the appropriate time, which calls for great commitment on the part of the owner.

House-training: Rottweiler puppies are particularly bright, and house-training is generally not a problem if owners are consistent and set their puppies up for success (see House-training 101, page 96)—but puppies will be puppies! There will be accidents on the carpet. There will be crates that must be cleaned out and little paws that need to be wiped. House-training takes effort and work and is part of raising a puppy.

Lifestyle changes: Puppies demand a lot of attention. If you're used to working long hours, sleeping in on Sunday mornings, dashing out

When this puppy loses his milk teeth and his adult teeth begin to come in, his desire to chew will be voracious.

for a bite to eat with friends, or taking off on weekend getaways, buying a puppy will put a screeching halt to your busy work and social life. Puppies need attention, love, and care. And, as he grows, he will require constant supervision—much like a curious toddler who is prone to get into trouble, except this canine toddler has the strength to really do some damage while he is investigating.

Expenses: Raising a puppy is not inexpensive. The purchase price of your Rottweiler puppy is the least of your concerns. Even if your Rottweiler puppy is healthy, he can easily run up more than $1,000 in expenses in his first year alone. Costs will include vaccinations, veterinary exams, training classes, food, and basic supplies. And, these figures don't even take into account the Oriental rug your Rottweiler might chew the fringe off one afternoon, or the dining room table leg that may be gnawed in half, or the three pairs of leather shoes that could end up shredded, or . . . well, you get the point!

When you weigh the pros and cons of raising a Rottweiler as a puppy, are you up to it? Or, is adopting an adult dog a scenario that might fit better into your current lifestyle? Perhaps, *no* Rottweiler is realistic at this time, and that's fine. The important point to realize is that puppy ownership isn't without its challenges. If you are capable and willing to handle these challenges, great. If not, wait until you are ready.

The key is that you go into this canine-human relationship with the attitude that you will make it work, no matter what bumps you hit in the road. With this approach, you will be successful.

Where to Find Your Rottweiler Puppy

As is the case with many things in life, when it comes to purchasing a Rottweiler puppy you often get what you pay for. The "bargain" pups selling for $200 in the newspaper are really no bargains at all in the long run, particularly with a breed such as the Rottweiler. Unfortunately, Rottweilers have been exploited by folks who just want to make some money off of a hot, canine fashion trend or those who feed on society's insecurities and try to sell a security system wrapped in black-and-rust coat. (You'd be better off with a real security system. Few people have the level of skill to work with a trained protection dog; the liability is high and the reliability is low.)

This is not to say that you can't find a Rottweiler puppy that will develop into a healthy, well-tempered, sociable family pet from a newspaper ad, backyard breeder, or a pet store. It's just that everything is stacked against you (and the puppy). Here's why.

The "Bargain" Puppy

With the bargain puppy, you have no guarantees. The breeding is generally haphazard, and often the only thought that has gone into the pairing is what male is available for the female that has just come into season. In other words, if you're expecting the puppy to grow up to look like the Rottweilers you've seen at shows or in books, forget it. The black-and-mahogany coloration may be the only thing that identifies this dog as a Rottweiler. Poorly bred Rottweilers are often leggy, houndy-looking, lighter eyed, longer muzzled, or basically just not what you'd expect to see.

Health: Looks aside, a more serious issue is the bargain puppy's health. It costs money to screen parents for hip dysplasia, elbow dysplasia, heart problems, vision, and other genetic diseases. Odds are the bargain puppy's parents haven't been screened or certified clear of any hereditary diseases. With the frequency at which many of these diseases can appear in the Rottweiler, taking a chance on a puppy from untested stock is a serious risk. You might very well spend two to three times more for the puppy's health care in her first year than you would have for the purchase price of a well-bred puppy from properly tested and screened parents. And, this is, of course, if the bargain puppy survives his first year. Some of the diseases that affect the Rottweiler are life threatening (see Common Diseases of the Rottweiler, Chapter Twelve).

Additionally, many bargain puppies have not received proper early health care, such as quality food and

Pet Store Puppies

Who can resist that puppy in the window? If you can't, then make sure you realize that pet store puppies are likely to fall prey to the same disadvantages as the "bargain" puppy. Rarely do these puppies come from generations of health-screened dogs, nor are the parents carefully selected for wonderful temperaments. Frequently, these puppies come from puppy brokers who purchase their puppies from puppy mills and puppy farmers. Though the puppies here will cost almost as much as those from a reputable breeder, the pet store will provide only a very limited, if any, guarantee.

Additionally, there is no Rottweiler expert at the pet store to help guide you in raising this puppy. And finally, for a breed that requires attention and socialization from an early age to develop into a well-balanced adult, the pet store puppy that is kept caged and in a window all day is already beginning life with a disadvantage.

If you succumb to the puppy in the window, make sure that you realize this is again a "buyer beware" type of situation.

mates. Or, they have a mother that is ill or is in a state of compromised health. These puppies begin life with health concerns that may or may not be able to be fully corrected later.

Temperament: Beyond conformation and health, there's temperament to consider. As has been mentioned previously, a good, calm temperament is absolutely essential to the success of a Rottweiler. Fearful or nervous Rottweilers are extremely dangerous as they are more likely to bite. Aggressive Rottweilers have no place in today's society for obvious reasons. The only Rottweiler that is acceptable is the one that is bred for a wonderful temperament. Puppy mills and pet stores that purchase dogs from puppy brokers or dealers are not concerned with temperament issues at all. Backyard breeders may have bred Ruby because "She's so sweet," to Onyx because "He's such a great dog," and indirectly bred nice temperaments. However, unless you're able to meet both parents of the puppy and find out for yourself that *both* are of sterling character, you are taking a chance.

No Guarantees: The bargain puppy can't be returned. If you discover a life-threatening illness or a rotten temperament, there's nothing you can do. It is truly a "buyer beware" type of situation.

Lack of Buyer Education: Finally, the seller of the bargain puppy doesn't care if you're capable of raising a Rottweiler or if you even have an understanding of the breed.

vaccinations. They may be infested with fleas and ticks, or be nearly consumed with internal parasites. Some don't even have a warm or clean place to sleep with their litter-

Many dogs fail in homes because the owner simply didn't understand what he or she was getting into. This holds true for the Rottweiler, too. This dog is not a dog for everyone, or even most people. It takes a special person to be a successful Rottweiler owner. Without any advice or screening on the part of the seller, many bargain puppies simply end up in the wrong hands. Or, perhaps they are placed in a good home, but when problems arise, the owner who is uneducated to the ways of the Rottweiler, fails to address the problems or handles them incorrectly and escalates the problem.

Reputable Breeders

So, now that you know where not to look for your puppy, how do you find a puppy that has come from quality breeding? And who is a reputable breeder anyway?

The reputable breeder is a person who is devoted to the Rottweiler breed. The breeder may be involved in showing or performance events, or both. He or she is usually a member of one of the national breed clubs, and may also be a member of a local or regional Rottweiler club. (Reputable breeders also support breed rescue.)

The reputable breeder does not breed for money or financial gain. He or she breeds only to better the breed and strives toward the elusive goal of perfection. Perfection for a Rottweiler is a dog that mirrors the breed standard, is the picture of health, possesses a flawless temperament, and that can compete in one or a variety of performance events. Dogs that have faults or possess hereditary conditions are not bred, no matter how handsome they are or how well loved. To do this would be to compromise the breed, and these breeders realize this.

What makes a great breeder is a reputable breeder who is willing to openly share his or her knowledge and serve as an advisor or mentor to his or her puppy buyers. A breeder may be doing everything correctly and may be producing highly acclaimed, topnotch Rottweilers, but if he or she is intimidating to the potential puppy buyer, the new owner is very likely never to tap into the wealth of knowledge that the experienced breeder possesses.

Great Rottweiler breeders can be found across the United States—that's the good news. The bad news is that according to some estimates, fewer than one in every ten breeders falls into the reputable category. Fortunately, there are many ways to seek out and find really good breeders who breed quality puppies and who are anxious to find wonderful homes for their Rottweilers. You just have to know where to look.

Breed rescue: "But I don't want an adult dog," you say. (Before you really decide this, check out Chapter Six: Adopting the Adult Rottweiler. You might just change your mind!) That's fine, but that's not why you're calling breed rescue. The reason you'll want to talk with these folks is because they know which breeders are wonderful to work with and they really know who to avoid. They can give you some great direction in your search and a few contacts to begin calling.

Rottweiler clubs: The American Rottweiler Club (ARC) provides breeder referrals to interested puppy buyers. The other national breed clubs, the United States Rottweiler Club (USRC) and the American Rottweiler Verein (ARV), can also provide referrals to breeders (for these addresses, see Useful Addresses and Literature, page 159).

Local breed clubs: The national breed clubs have many regional and local breed clubs as members. To find a Rottweiler club in your area, check with the national club. If there is a club near you, call the club's contact person, usually the club secretary, and ask this person to direct you to a breeder in your area.

All-breed dog clubs: You may not have a Rottweiler breed club in your area, but you might have an all-breed dog club. Contact the corresponding secretary of this club and find out if he or she can refer you to some reputable Rottweiler members. These members may not be breeding themselves, but they may be able to refer you to someone they recognize as a top breeder.

Local training clubs: Where there's obedience, tracking, and agility, there are going to be Rottweilers. If you have a training club in your area, visit the club and ask owners and trainers for some referrals to Rottweiler breeders.

Dog shows: A good place to talk to experienced owners and breeders is at a dog show. For a schedule of upcoming events, check the AKC's web site. At shows one of the best places to talk with owners and breeders is not at the ring itself, but rather in the sea of RVs in the parking lot. Here the atmosphere is more laid back and you can find lots of Rottweilers and their owners (and a lot of handlers) with their dogs. Away from the stress of judging, most people will welcome your questions and will be happy to show you their dogs and "talk Rottweiler."

Veterinarians: At the very least, your veterinarian will know who takes care of their Rottweilers and who doesn't. He or she will also be adept at recognizing dogs with good temperaments and those with fearful, nervous, or aggressive tendencies. If a breeder is recommended by a trusted veterinarian, you can be pretty confident that the individual is reputable.

What You Can Expect from a Breeder

Before you make your first phone call to a respected breeder, there are a few things you should be prepared for and should expect. First, that you will be grilled. Generally, you'll be questioned in an interested and friendly way, but the breeder will want to know about you, how much you know about dogs, what types of dogs you owned (and how they died), what you understand about Rottweilers, and what your level of commitment to a dog is.

Don't be put off by inquisitiveness or a battery of questions from the breeder! Rottweiler breeders have a single goal in mind when it comes to prospective owners: They want good, permanent homes for their Rottweilers. They don't want an owner to fail with a puppy, and they don't want a puppy to fail in his new home.

Discerning breeders: Some Rottweiler breeders will not sell to people who have never owned a Rottweiler before, single men (who are sure to meet a single woman at some point and may put the woman before the dog), people who live in small homes, or any number of other predetermined criteria.

Do not be discouraged if you are turned down by a breeder for one of these reasons. There are many very good breeders who place their puppies on an individual basis. These breeders recognize that if you have the qualities it takes to own a Rottweiler, and the commitment needed to care for a dog, then you will make a very good home for one of their puppies.

The breeder's screening: After you've talked with the breeder, you will be invited to visit his or her dogs and possibly some of the puppies, if there are puppies available at the time. What the breeder wants to see is how you and your family—if you have a spouse and children—react and interact with the puppies as well as the adult Rottweilers. This is also a great opportunity to ask the breeder questions about his or her dogs, how the breeder breeds, what the

breeder's dogs have accomplished, such as conformation and performance titles, and for what types of health conditions the breeder screens. Ask the breeder for references, such as other people who have purchased puppies from the breeder, and call these people. Find out how satisfied they have been with their dogs and the breeder.

After you've met with the breeder and have passed muster, if he or she does not have any puppies available at the moment, which is very likely considering that many breeders do not raise more than a litter a year at most, you will most likely be put on a waiting list for future puppies. You may be asked for a deposit to hold a puppy; this is not unusual.

When the litter arrives: When the litter arrives, the breeder will call for you to come out and take a look at the puppies. You may be able to select a puppy at five or six weeks, but since they are still at a critical developmental stage with their littermates at this time, you will not be allowed to take home your puppy until he is at least eight weeks old.

Paperwork: An experienced breeder will require that you sign a purchase agreement. This agreement is a binding contract that spells out exactly what the breeder is selling you, as well as your responsibilities to the puppy once he is in your possession. For example, a contract may contain the guarantee that if the puppy is determined by a veterinarian to have a serious illness or condition within a few days after purchase, or a serious hereditary disease within a reasonable amount of time, that the breeder will replace the puppy with another puppy of equal or greater quality, or refund the purchase price of the puppy.

In turn, the contract can be expected to contain a clause that requires a pet quality puppy to be spayed or neutered by the age of six months, and a stipulation that registration (usually a limited registration in this case) will be withheld until proof of the altering is provided to the breeder.

Contracts for show or performance prospects may call for a reevaluation of the dog's conformation and/or capabilities at a later date. If the Rottweiler is deemed unsuitable for breeding at this point, the breeder may retain the right to require that the dog be altered at this time. Contracts for potential

Limited Registrations

A limited registration is a type of registration in which the dog is registered with the American Kennel Club (AKC) and can compete in non-conformation events, such as tracking, agility, or obedience. The registration is "limited" because the dog cannot be bred. If a dog with a limited registration is bred, the AKC will not register the dog's puppies. Limited registration papers are bordered in orange rather than the full registration papers, which are bordered in blue.

show or performance Rottweilers may also require co-ownership with the breeder.

Note: Be sure you understand exactly what co-ownership entails: (i.e., the right of the breeder to select mates, to choose the pick of the litter, to control entry decisions in shows, etc.) before you agree to co-owning a dog. Co-owning a dog may be a great way to own a dog that would not have been possible otherwise; however, if your goals are not the same as those of your co-owner, the situation could be difficult.

Finding a Puppy That's Best for You

You've found a tremendous breeder, you have a deposit on a puppy, you understand the terms of the breeder's contract, and now the litter is here. You walk into the breeder's home and are met by ten black-and-mahogany bundles of fur that are tumbling over each other to greet and play with you. How on earth are you going to decide which puppy will be your companion for the next decade or more?

First of all, though you may be greeted by up to a dozen Rottweiler puppies, many will not be available. Other puppy buyers who have also placed deposits on puppies may have already selected or had a puppy selected by the breeder. Realistically, perhaps half of the litter may be available for you to choose from, but there are ways to narrow your choices down before you even see the puppies.

Pick Your Purpose

If a Rottweiler is well bred, he will be healthy, of sound conformation, and possessing the potential for a stellar temperament. Any puppy meeting these criteria will make an excellent companion dog. If you know you want to do more with your puppy than raise him to be a good pet, then you will want to discuss these goals with your breeder. Your breeder will then be able to better help you choose a puppy that will meet your expectations.

For example, if you think you'd like to show your Rottweiler, then a show-quality puppy is a must. If you aren't experienced with the breed, then you will need to rely on your breeder's expertise in helping you find a show quality puppy. Keep in mind, however, that determining exactly how a puppy will turn out is part experience, part gut feeling, and part luck. In other words, *there are no guarantees.*

Also, if you want a show-quality puppy, expect to pay more. Some breeders will charge the same fees for both pet- and show-quality puppies; however, it is quite common for show-quality puppies to sell for 50 percent more or even double the asking price of pet-quality puppies.

Performance: Rottweilers that do well in performance events generally have enthusiasm, energy, and a high prey drive.

When you visit the puppies, carefully observe not only the health and temperaments of the puppies, but that of the puppies' parents, too.

Note: The use of the word "prey" should not be misconstrued as the dog having killer instincts or a high "predatory" drive. A high prey drive is recognized by an intense drive to pursue, catch, play, and retrieve balls. A *predatory* drive is actually quite different—and dangerous—and is indicated by catching and killing small animals.

When choosing a puppy for a sport, you'll want the healthiest dog possible and, because your dog will be called upon to perform strenuous activities, he must be clear of hip and elbow problems and heart disease. A pedigree with up to three generations of dogs tested for these diseases is an excellent hedge against hereditary diseases, but it is not a guarantee.

If you have a particular sport in mind, such as tracking, agility, obedience, or Schutzhund, be sure to discuss this with your breeder in

Not a Sign of Quality

AKC papers alone do not signify quality breeding. The reason for this is that in the United States any Rottweiler with AKC papers can be bred to any other Rottweiler with papers. The dogs used for breeding could be of poor or even disqualifying conformation, ill tempered, and potentially possessing the genetic capacity to pass on serious and even life-threatening diseases to their offspring. In other words, for a Rottweiler to be registered with the AKC there are no requirements other than for the puppy to have parents that are registered with the AKC.

However, there are many ways in which the outstanding breeding practices of American breeders are recognized. Championships, performance titles, and certifications of health screenings and tests are just a few of the ways American breeders are working toward maintaining exacting standards themselves.

Breeding for good conformation will be indicated with a pedigree that is filled with champions—not just one or two here and there. Breeding for working abilities can be indicated by a variety of performance titles, such as agility, obedience, herding, and tracking. And, breeding for good temperaments can be recorded with a Canine Good Citizen title (see Activities, pages 155–156), though many of the performance titles are also good indicators, but not proof, that a dog comes from a line of steady temperaments.

advance and have him or her help you in your decision.

Certified Pedigrees

The American Kennel Club (AKC) issues certified pedigrees that are affixed with the seal of the AKC. These official pedigrees list four generations of an individual dog or puppy's ancestors. Included in the pedigree is each dog's name with all AKC titles, AKC registration number, date of birth, the Orthopedic Foundation for Animals (OFA) rating (excellent, good, fair, etc.) if available, and the dog's color (black-and-tan, black-and-brown, black-and-rust, or black-and-mahogany).

• Dogs appearing in the pedigree that are in Germany will have an ADRK registration number.

• Dogs that have been imported from Germany into the United States will have an AKC registration number that notes the dog's country of origin in parenthesis following the dog's color.

• Because the AKC does not recognize Schutzhund titles or any other international titles, such as temperament and conformation ratings, the German Rottweilers and German imports will not have any of this valuable information appearing with their names on the AKC's certified pedigree. Schutzhund titles achieved in the United States are also not listed on the AKC pedigrees. (Breeders may provide this information on their own, unofficial pedigrees.)

Male or Female?

Does the sex of your Rottweiler puppy make any difference to you? If you are interested in showing and eventually breeding your Rottweiler, then most breeders recommend selecting a show-quality female puppy.

If you are interested in a good companion, both males and females are good choices. Often, pet owners assume that the female is the sweeter and gentler of the sexes. This is not necessarily true. As one breeder put it: Males will fight with each other until they determine who is the boss and one will back down. Females, on the other hand, will often fight to the death. Hmmm. Sweet and gentle? Females can be very sweet, but they are still Rottweilers.

• Females can be just as protective as males.

• Females will attempt to lead if the owner does not provide leadership.

• Some females may have a lower tolerance to children's antics than a male dog and a greater tendency to want to "correct" children as she would a misbehaving pup. Of course, this is not true of all females, but it can be a tendency.

What about males? Some prospective owners worry that a male dog may be more difficult to handle . . . Again, this isn't necessarily so. Many owners and breeders swear that the "boys" are the devoted, loving, extremely tolerant dogs. For many owners, males are preferred to females.

• Males have the advantage in competitive sports because they never come in season.

• Of course, though male Rottweilers don't come in season, an unaltered male is *always* "in season" for a potential mate, creating its own unique difficulties.

• Males are larger than females. Their sheer size alone can be difficult to manage before the puppy is even full grown.

What puppy—male or female—is best for you may depend on what you are looking for in a dog and what the individual temperaments of the puppies in the litter are. Remember: Ultimately, every Rottweiler is unique.

When You Meet the Puppies

Whether you are looking for a specific type of puppy or just wanting a great companion, you'll want to look at your potential picks very carefully. If you haven't already met the puppies' parents, you'll want to do this now, if possible. Researchers say the best way to guarantee a good temperament is to ensure that both parents have ideal temperaments. If the female was bred to a male from another breeder, you may not be able to see both dogs at this time. If this is the case, ask for the stud dog owner's name and phone number and call him or her.

When visiting with the puppies, look carefully at the surroundings in which the puppy is raised. If you've been careful in your search for a good breeder, you'll find that the puppies are frequently whelped in the owner's home in a special whelping box that is warm and dry. Any sign that the puppies are raised in filthy or less than desirable circumstances is an indicator that the breeder has fallen short in his or her job of caring for the puppies.

General Impressions

When looking at the puppies, begin by observing first and handling second. In both instances, you are looking for any signs of ill health. If you are purchasing your puppy from an experienced and reputable breeder, you should find the puppies to be in perfect health. Even so, it is wise to check.

• Watch the puppy's movement. Any limps or other awkward movement at this early age could indicate either a recent injury, a serious developmental problem, or even disease.

• Examine the pup's symmetry. The puppy's legs should be the same length, and ears and eyes should be balanced. Again, anything outside of what is considered "normal" could indicate a problem.

• Feel the puppy's coat. It should be thick and clean. Missing patches of fur could indicate ringworm, mange, or another skin condition.

• Look for signs of fleas and ticks, such as irritated patches of skin, scratching, redness, pustules caused by flea or tick bites, or the flea or tick itself. Healthy puppies that have been kept in clean surroundings should not have these parasites.

• Examine the puppy's skin. Feel for any bumps and look for flaky or dry skin. If the puppy doesn't have smooth, supple skin, it could be a sign of ill health.

• Check the puppy's eyes. Do they look bright or do they appear dull or cloudy? Are there any signs of weeping or oozing from the eyes? Any of these signs may indicate something is amiss.

• Keep an eye open for other problems. Discharges from any of the puppy's orifices (eyes, nose, ears, genitals, and anus) could also indicate that the puppy is ill. Diarrhea and blood in the stool are red flags for a variety of illnesses and parasites, including parvovirus, worms, and giardia.

Temperament Testing

There are many different variations of temperament testing that have been designed by dog trainers and animal behaviorists to help determine a puppy's predisposition to various character traits. These tests look to see if the puppy is dominant or submissive, if he enjoys being handled, and if he shows normal inquisitiveness or is fearful of new stimuli.

For the most part, the tests can be helpful in determining the traits of a puppy. The Rottweiler puppy, however, invariably tests as being dominant or not submissive. *This is not abnormal, unusual, or cause for alarm!* The Rottweiler by nature is not a submissive breed. It will not generally submit to an alpha roll—a roll onto the back in a submissive posture—or allow scruffing—grabbing the puppy by the scruff of the neck. This is one of the traits of the breed.

With this understanding, there are also levels of dominance within the definition of "dominant" itself. A first-time Rottweiler owner would be wise not to choose a puppy that is extremely dominant or the most dominant puppy in the litter. These pups are not bad dogs; they just require an owner who is very experienced in training and handling them and who can shape them into role model adults.

One temperament that should be avoided is the fearful or nervous puppy. This puppy will require a very special home with an extremely skilled and dedicated trainer to develop the Rottweiler into a well-adjusted canine. As mentioned before, fearfulness is the top reason for dog bites, and a bite from a fearful Rottweiler is a serious issue. Though you may feel sorry for the shy puppy, he is not a good choice.

On another note, if you notice that there are several fearful or shy puppies in a litter, you would be well advised to pass on all the puppies. A litter with many timid Rottweilers is not normal and could be an indicator of poor breeding.

Making the Selection

So many puppies and they're all so cute! How do you decide? If you've gone over the puppies physically and they all look great, just sit and wait. Usually you will find yourself being drawn to one particular puppy, and the puppy to you. The breeder can also help you make your decision; knowing your lifestyle and the individual personalities of the puppies can help to make a perfect match.

If, however, you aren't drawn to any of the puppies or are apprehensive for any reason, don't make a decision now. Wait. Think about it. Perhaps even wait for another litter. If you are not absolutely taken by your Rottweiler puppy and thoroughly committed to his care for the next decade or more, then now is not the time to purchase a puppy.

Remember: When you bring your Rottweiler puppy home, you are filling the role of his mother, littermates, and even the breeder. It is your responsibility to raise him properly and provide the best possible training and care that you can. If you take this responsibility seriously, your Rottweiler will reward you with a depth of devotion that you may have never experienced with any other pet.

Chapter Six

Adopting the Adult Rottweiler

Not all dog owners are cut out to raise a puppy. Puppies are cute and there are many advantages to raising a Rottweiler; however, these canine kids can be very challenging. As noted in Chapter Five, puppies have to be trained, socialized, and house-trained, and the job of damage control during the teething phase can be daunting,

Most adult dogs can bond just as deeply with a new owner as the dog that lives in the same home from puppyhood.

particularly when that puppy is a Rottweiler!

If raising a puppy seems a bit too much for you right now, or if you're perhaps interested in "making a difference" in a Rottweiler's life, you might be interested in learning more about adopting an adult Rottweiler. As with buying a puppy, there are both benefits and challenges to adopting and raising an adult Rottweiler. If you carefully choose your source for an adult Rottweiler and make the commitment to help the adult dog adjust to a new life, the benefits generally far outweigh any challenges you might encounter.

Benefits of the Adopted Rottweiler

A common misconception is that Rottweilers that are surrendered to shelters and rescues are problem dogs (see Breed Rescues, page 60). Certainly, there are problem Rottweilers that are surrendered; however, if the behavior problems are significant, for instance, if the Rottweiler is aggressive toward people or has a history of biting, the dog is not placed and is subsequently euthanized. Thousands of Rottweilers are given up each year. Those that cannot be rehomed actually make up a small percentage, according to breed rescue workers. In fact, many Rottweilers that are rescued from horrendous conditions remain trusting of humans and eager to begin a new life with someone who will love them and treat them with great care.

In addition to saving a dog's life and giving her a second chance, dog adoption has many other advantages, including knowing your dog's temperament and health, and avoiding many of the challenges of raising a puppy.

Knowing What You Have

In addition to knowing just how your Rottweiler will look as an adult (she *is* an adult), adopting a rescued Rottweiler offers several ofther benefits.

Health: It is possible to adopt a very healthy, problem-free, adult Rottweiler. The majority of rescue dogs are healthy and relatively problem-free. But even if the dog has health problems—and often these can be screened for in adults but not in puppies—the adopter is aware of the health problems and is capable of making a decision of whether or not he or she can handle the dog's situation *before* making an emotional and financial commitment to the dog.

Temperament: According to a recent survey, the most critical concern among adopters of *all* breeds of dogs is whether the adopted dog has a good temperament. The concern is probably more weighty with prospective Rottweiler adopters who are keenly aware of the liability and potential damage an unstable Rottweiler could inflict on both family members and strangers.

Breed rescue workers point out that if an adopter works through an experienced and reputable Rottweiler rescue group—those people who *know* Rottweilers—adopting an adult dog that has been fostered in a home and thoroughly temperament tested may actually be less of a risk than raising a puppy. With an adult dog, there's no guessing what the final outcome will be: What you see is what you get. If the Rottweiler is excellent with children, you'll know that. If the Rottweiler chases cats or can't go into another home with other pets, you'll know that, too. You'll know if she is aggressive with other dogs, or if she's extremely tolerant. If she's full of energy at the age of three, you'll know you've got a real fireball on your hands and this isn't likely to be something she'll outgrow anytime soon.

Avoiding Puppy Problems

As mentioned briefly in this chapter, one of the most attractive reasons to consider adopting the adult Rottweiler is that as an adult, the dog has outgrown many puppy "vices."

Chewing: The adult Rottweiler will still like to chew, and as a breed,

It is a testament to the Rottweiler breed that so many dogs can be neglected and even abused and still be eager to trust and devote themselves to a new owner.

Want to Compete?

If you are adopting a Rottweiler and are interested in obedience, agility, or any number of sports, you can participate! A purebred Rottweiler can compete in most events *without* American Kennel Club (AKC) papers. All that is needed is an Indefinite Listing Privilege (ILP) number, for which you can apply to AKC (see page 159).

Rottweilers are notoriously tough on their toys. However, the urge to chew will not be as voracious as during the time when a puppy is teething. So, as long as you keep your Rottweiler well supplied with safe and healthy chewing options, you should be able to avoid the search-and-destroy days of puppy teething.

House-training: Many rescued Rottweilers are already house-trained. Others may simply need a refresher course, and this can be accomplished quite quickly and effortlessly with crate training (see House-training 101, page 96). Even Rottweilers that have spent most of their lives in a backyard with no house-training can readily be taught that the house is their kennel and the yard is their relief station. Adult dogs have control over their bodily functions; puppies are often four months or older before they begin to gain complete control. Adult dogs can also "last" longer than young puppies, making house-training a bit easier.

Ready to Train

Finally, adult Rottweilers often have some basic command training (many dogs know how to sit on command). Even those that don't can be readily trained. As Joan Sweeney, founder and director of the Wisconsin Rottweiler Rescue notes, "Every time the leash goes on the dog (for training), the owner is telling the dog, 'We're a team.' This is the dream of most Rottweilers!"

Challenges of the Adopted Rottweiler

In most cases, a Rottweiler that has been carefully screened and temperament tested can be placed in a home that meets her needs, and the adjustment period goes off without a hitch. In other cases, the Rottweiler may come with some baggage from her previous life that may take a longer adjustment period and a patient owner. In some cases, the behaviors may be more complex, requiring an experienced owner who is able to work with the dog to overcome her foibles and develop into a well-adjusted dog.

Fear of the Unknown

Perhaps the greatest question regarding an adult Rottweiler is, what has this dog been through and how will these experiences affect how she behaves today, tomorrow, or next month? With many Rottweilers, the past will never be known. When a dog is unceremoniously chained to a shelter's door after hours, unless someone recognizes the dog and knows the previous owner, little will ever be known about the dog except that she is now unwanted.

Sometimes what *is* known about a dog is actually false. Shelter workers say that owners will often drop off a dog, and to save face will fabricate a story about the dog to justify why they couldn't handle her anymore. Shelters say this happens more often than the reverse, in which an owner might say a dog is much better than she actually is to help her be adopted.

Lack of history is a concern; however, if the shelter or rescue is equipped to fully examine, observe,

The Deepest Bond

Some owners hesitate to adopt an adult dog because they believe that the human-canine bond can never be as deep "the second time around." Rescue volunteers say this is a common misconception. In fact, some say that a dog that has had little love often bonds as deeply, *if not deeper,* with the person who shows him the attention and care he so desperately needs.

As long as the dog still trusts humans, there is no reason why a close bond can't be formed between the rescued dog's new and permanent owner. Given a chance, rescued Rottweilers can make tremendous companions.

and test the Rottweiler for temperament flaws, minor quirks, and even preferences, much can be learned about the dog. The more experienced the rescue or shelter, the more accurate the analysis of the dog's temperament will be, and the less likely you will have any unpleasant surprises.

Health

Though an adult dog can be tested for many life-threatening illnesses, many rescued Rottweilers have not had the benefit of good breeding to help screen out hereditary diseases, nor have they received much, if any, veterinary care. Dogs in many areas have heartworm and have to undergo treatment before

Rottweiler rescues are careful to screen for temperament, as well as health.

themselves until the dog is much older, such as some heart conditions or thyroid problems.

Rehoming a rescued Rottweiler could become a costly experience. Fortunately, the dog will have received a complete veterinary exam and often, any serious illnesses will have already been treated. In cases of chronic illnesses, often, these conditions are already known. So, even though it may be more costly to treat this dog during her lifetime, at least the owner enters the adoption fully aware of the situation.

House-training

Though house-training is generally easier and goes much more quickly when working with an adult dog, when the adult Rottweiler makes a mistake—it's a big one! Enough said.

Training

Working with 130 pounds (59 kg) of muscle, bone, and attitude can be much more challenging than working with 30 pounds (14 kg) of malleable puppy. Even the strongest person would be hard pressed to prevent being dragged by a Rottweiler on a mission. Fortunately, with positive reinforcement training—and using food lures to get a dog to sit and lie down—training an adult Rottweiler is possible. There are also new training tools, such as the head halter, that allows even petite individuals to control an adult Rottweiler and be able to work on training skills.

they can be placed. Other dogs may suffer from non-life-threatening illnesses that are chronic in nature, such as allergies. Still others may have diseases that don't manifest

Adopted Rottweilers and Kids

It is particularly important if you've adopted an adult Rottweiler and you are introducing this dog into a family with children that the dog has been carefully screened for her behavior around children. (Because of the dog's sheer size alone, accidents can happen quickly and with serious consequences.) Even if the dog comes with sterling credentials, she must still prove to you that she is as perfect as her evaluators say she is. In other words, work with her carefully until over the weeks, months, and years she has become fully integrated as a family member.

Also, make sure your children know the rules of dog care. Your Rottweiler is a dog and can be expected to tolerate only so much. Children must know and must be able to be counted upon to treat the adopted dog with kindness and respect and follow these basic rules:

• Don't tease, poke, pinch, or otherwise hurt the Rottweiler.

• The dog's crate is not a playhouse or something to share with the dog.

• Wake the dog by softly calling her name rather than petting or shaking her.

• If the dog has something in her mouth, never try to take it away. You'll want to teach your dog to give up anything she is carrying when you ask her to, but this is not something the dog should be *expected* to

do without working on this skill. Resource guarding is a common trait.

• Don't roughhouse or wrestle with the dog. The Rottweiler *will* win and your child will get hurt.

• Loud screaming, shrieks, and running up and down and flapping arms and legs can alarm a Rottweiler or confuse him into thinking that someone is being injured. Your children need to realize this and you need to

When adopting the adult Rottweiler through a skilled and experienced source, you may not know the dog's exact past or his pedigree, but you will know that he has a great temperament.

run interference if your child gets into an argument or tussle with another child in the presence of the dog.

• Respect the Rottweiler and she will be your faithful companion.

And finally, always provide close supervision when your children are interacting with the dog. If you can't supervise *closely* (this means you're right on top of the situation, not watching from the kitchen window while they're together in the backyard), then *separate.* If you can't adequately keep your kids away from your Rottweiler or your Rottweiler from your kids, then don't get a dog. Period.

Adult Rottweiler Sources

The key to a successful adoption, and making that perfect match between dog and owner, is to go through an adoption program that has had extensive experience with Rottweilers and knows how to assess a Rottweiler's behaviors and potential as a rehomed companion. Experienced rescue organization people will not only be accurate in their evaluation of the dog, but they will also be able to provide invaluable assistance during the entire time you are working to adjust your dog to her new home.

There are several ways in which you can adopt an adult Rottweiler, and all have their benefits and drawbacks. Which avenue you choose to

follow to adopt your Rottweiler may very well hinge on what is available in your community.

Breed Rescues

A breed rescue is a nonprofit national, regional, or local organization that devotes itself to rescuing one breed of dog. (Shelters and pounds rescue all breeds and mixes thereof.) Rottweiler breed rescues, therefore, are devoted entirely to rescuing and rehoming Rottweilers. Rottweiler breed rescues are generally founded and run by extremely knowledgeable and experienced Rottweiler breeders, trainers, or owners. Often, directors of these rescues are members of one of the national breed clubs and/or a local or regional club.

Breed rescues will frequently work with a dog from several weeks to a month or more before they will place the dog with an approved family. During this time, the Rottweiler is bathed, parasites (inside and out) are removed, and the dog is given a complete veterinary exam. If the dog is healthy she is spayed, or neutered if a male. If the Rottweiler needs treatment for a condition or illness, this is also begun. The dogs are brought up to date on their vaccinations and tattooed for permanent identification and registration. They are also given obedience training and a lot of handling and attention.

Once the rescue organization feels the Rottweiler is in good health and of sound temperament, the dog is available for adoption. Most rescues try to recruit applicants for rescued dogs so that they can place dogs as they become available. Sometimes, however, some dogs may have to wait a little longer to find a "perfect" home.

If you are considering adopting an adult Rottweiler, you will go through much of the same processes involved as you would if you were considering buying a puppy through a responsible breeder. As with the responsible breeder, the sometimes detailed process is simply because the rescue wants to make sure the right Rottweiler goes into the right home, and that home is a permanent, loving one.

If you are adopting a Rottweiler from a Rottweiler rescue, you can expect the following:

• Application/screening: You will most likely have to fill out an application that will include information as to your past experiences with dogs and Rottweilers, your current lifestyle, your expectations for the new dog, and your commitment to rehoming an adult Rottweiler.

• Home visit: Many rescues will follow-up your application with a telephone interview, and possibly a visit to your home.

• Rescue visit: Virtually all Rottweiler rescues will require potential adopters to come to their homes and visit adult Rottweilers. This is to observe how you and your family members get along with adult dogs, and to give you a chance to see what it takes to be a successful Rottweiler owner.

Seized by animal control, this Rottweiler had survived in a cage for more than a year, eating cracked corn every other day and tolerating daily abuse from his owner. After a month of nurturing at Second Chance Rottweiler Rescue in Evansville, Indiana, "München" was placed with a loving family.

• Waiting list: If all goes well, you will be put on a waiting list to adopt a Rottweiler. As potential matches come in to the rescue, you will be notified and given the opportunity to meet the dog.

• Contracts: Once the match has been made, you will be required to sign a contract, stating that if you must ever give up the dog, you must

Can't Adopt? Consider Helping!

1. Foster homes. If you're experienced with Rottweilers, you might consider offering your home and experience as a foster home to a rescued Rottweiler.

2. "In-kind" donations. Rescues are always in need of collars, leashes, food and water dishes, crates, pads, food, and even coupons for food.

3. Cash: It takes money to run a rescue. A cash donation to a Rottweiler rescue is tax deductible (if the rescue has a nonprofit status with the IRS) and it will go to a good cause.

4. Personal time. Rescues can frequently use volunteers to help with a wide variety of jobs.

5. Special skills/services. Do you have a special skill you might be able to share with a rescue? Call your local or regional organization to see if you can help.

contact the rescue. Also, if you mistreat, neglect, or abuse the Rottweiler, the rescue retains the right to take the dog back.

Breeders

Sometimes a breeder will have an excellent Rottweiler that would make a great companion dog. Perhaps the dog was returned, or the breeder may have held onto the dog, thinking she might develop into a show prospect but didn't. If you're looking for a Rottweiler, it never hurts to check with good breeders in your area to find out if someone might just have an adult in their kennel or home that they want to place.

Puppy mill warning: Beware of one source of adult Rottweilers—the puppy mill or puppy farmer. When a bitch can no longer breed, these disreputable breeders will try to unload her. Because dogs raised in cages in disgusting conditions rarely receive any human contact, a dog from this situation may be both physically and mentally ill.

If you find an adult that you suspect is being sold by an operation such as this, call your local Humane Society or contact your local police. Every municipality handles dog abuse and puppy mill cases differently, but these contacts will be able to tell you exactly how to file a complaint or get someone involved to investigate the situation.

Whatever you do, don't remain silent! All dogs deserve at least a chance at a decent life; puppy mill operators don't offer this as an option, *ever.*

Shelters and Pounds

Until breed rescues began to become popular in the 1990s, most people searching to adopt an adult dog turned to the local shelters and pounds. Today, you can still find a great Rottweiler from these organizations. However, be aware that many nonprofit shelters and pounds, cannot afford all the services that are necessary to screen and place a dog such as the Rottweiler.

In shelters and pounds that are staffed with experienced, caring personnel, adopting an adult Rottweiler can be a safe and satisfying experience. These folks take the time to work with the dogs daily and really get to know their strengths and weaknesses. They also screen owners as carefully as the breed rescues, and they provide training classes in their facilities, as well as behavior hotlines to help solve problems immediately. These are tremendous facilities and they *do* exist around the country.

Other facilities do not have the time, money, or staff to offer these services. They're doing their best to keep the dogs warm, clean, and fed. If this type of facility is in your area, be sure to bring an experienced Rottweiler breeder or trainer with you. When a Rottweiler—or any dog for that matter—is thrown into a strange and chaotic environment, it can be very difficult to see the dog's true temperament, and you may be able to see very little of the dog's character until she is removed from the shelter situation.

Enough words of caution cannot be expressed when adopting an adult Rottweiler from a situation in which the dog has not been fostered for a significant period of time and temperament tested. If you undertake an adoption such as this, make sure you are prepared for anything, never compromise the safety of your children or anyone else's, and work with professionals. Seek out experienced Rottweiler trainers and breeders to help you through your dog's adjustment period and identify any potential behavior problems.

Learning to Trust Again

For many adult Rottweilers, learning to trust people again and realizing that someone does care for them is all that it takes for these dogs to blossom. Perhaps they may be a bit reserved at first as they learn the ropes, meet new people, and learn new routines, but as soon as they have life figured out and are comfortable, the big clown will emerge. That's when you know you've made a difference.

Chapter Seven

Preparing for the New Arrival

Whether you're adopting an adult dog or purchasing a puppy, don't wait until the day you bring home your Rottweiler to get things ready. You'll want this day to spend time with your new puppy or dog, not running around frantically trying to find the right food and a crate that fits. With a little planning, you can even shop to make more affordable choices, selecting products that are economical, meet your Rottweiler's needs, yet don't break the bank.

What to Do in Advance

Veterinarian

Even if your puppy isn't due for another round of vaccinations or your adopted Rottweiler has just had a complete veterinary exam, you should still schedule an appointment for a general exam with your veterinarian. (If you currently don't have a veterinarian, see Selecting a Veterinarian, page 112.) You will want this trusted, professional opinion to confirm that you have indeed purchased a Rottweiler that is healthy and without any serious behavioral problems. At this time, your veterinarian will schedule the remaining vaccinations for your puppy.

If you have purchased your puppy from a questionable source or adopted an adult from a shelter that doesn't provide physical and behavioral screening services, this first visit to the veterinarian is even more crucial. For the well-being of your Rottweiler, and for the health of other pets at home and family members—some diseases are zoonotic and can be passed from dog to human—you'll want to make sure that your Rottweiler is free of diseases and parasites before you bring him home.

Cleanup time: If you are adopting an adult dog from a shelter and the dog is very dirty or infested with fleas and/or ticks, you will want to make your first stop at the veterinarian's office for an exam, and your second stop at the grooming shop for a complete cleanup. Once your Rottweiler is given a clean bill of health and is all dirt and parasite free, then you can introduce him to your home.

Training Classes

Remember to register for a training class. Puppy training classes, also frequently referred to as puppy kindergarten or puppy preschool, are designed for puppies only. These classes are very popular and fill up quickly, so you will want to be sure to locate a good training school and reserve a spot in an upcoming session as soon as possible—after consulting with your veterinarian.

Depending on the risks in your area for exposure to deadly diseases such as parvovirus (see page 114), your veterinarian may ask you not to expose your puppy to large numbers of puppies and dogs until he or she feels your puppy has developed an immunity to these diseases. This could be as early as 12 weeks, or as late as 16 to 20 weeks. For this reason, you'll need to find out first from your veterinarian what age he or she recommends to safely take your puppy into a class setting, and then register for a class beginning around that time.

Adopters of adult Rottweilers need to reserve a spot in a training class as soon as possible, too. Most adult dogs can use a refresher course in basic commands, and all can use the experience as an avenue to bond with their new owner. Remember: Give these guys a job to do—any job—and they will respond with gusto. It's what makes them happy. And a happy, *trained* adult Rottweiler makes for a happy owner.

Supplies for Your New Rottweiler

The initial purchases required for a new puppy or dog can take a toll on the checkbook. Fortunately, many of these purchases will last for years and, as mentioned previously, if you shop around and talk to other owners, you can get more for your money by finding products that work well with Rottweilers and hold up to the physical abuse a big dog can give them.

Make sure that one of the first things you get for your Rottweiler is a good, sturdy collar and readable identification tags.

Collar

Your Rottweiler will need a good, sturdy collar. This collar should *not* be a choke chain or martingale collar that tightens when pulled: This is a serious choking hazard. Even when you begin training your Rottweiler, particularly if you begin training with a young puppy, you will not need a choke chain. Progressive training schools use only flat buckle collars—no more "yank and yelp" training!

If you've purchased a puppy, a nylon or heavy cotton web collar that can expand several sizes can save you from having to buy several sizes of collars. These collars generally have plastic snap closures. But be careful—the plastic snap is the weakest part of the collar. Make sure the snap is durable, so your Rottweiler doesn't pull hard one day and break away.

The flat buckle collar is another good choice and can be adjusted, depending on the number of holes. A long flap should not be left extending beyond the buckle; this extra piece can easily get caught and possibly strangle your dog.

Caution: Rambunctious puppies have been known to strangle themselves in their crates. For this reason you should be very careful to remove the collar from the puppy before he is put in his crate if you will not be able to supervise him.

Leash

One of the most frequent mistakes new Rottweiler puppy owners make is to go out and buy a big, burly leash with a 2-pound (.91 kg) clip on the end of it. (O.K., maybe 2 pounds is a slight exaggeration, but you get the idea.) Sure, you'll need a sturdy leash for a full-grown dog, but that heavy clip on a puppy is going to be a distraction.

So, for young puppies, purchase a light leash that is suitable and appropriate for the puppy's size. As the puppy grows, you can move up to a sturdier leash.

As for what type of leash to select, you can purchase leashes that are nylon, cotton web, and leather. The cotton feels best to the hand, but the nylon may last longer. Leather leashes are great for training, but unless you can keep it away from your Rottweiler at all other times, anything made of leather is too irresistible not to chew.

As for chain leashes, avoid them. These leashes are terrible to try to hold—imagine a cold, icy day as you try to gather up a chain link leash barehanded—and they portray the *wrong* image of this breed.

Crate

A crate is an invaluable tool that can be used in house-training, separation anxiety, and simply preventing accidents or destruction that might occur when you can't be home. There are many styles and sizes to choose from, each with their own benefits and drawbacks. For Rottweilers, the best choice is usually a wire mesh crate that enables the Rottweiler to see everything that is going on around him. Also, placement of the crate is key with a Rottweiler: The crate should be in the center of the household's activity so that your Rottweiler never feels left out and can be with his family, even when in the crate.

For more detailed information on sizing a crate and how to use it for house-training, see Chapter Nine.

Travel Harness

If you can't fit a crate in your car, you'll need to invest in a travel harness.

There are many different manufacturers of special travel harnesses that can be buckled to a seat belt in the backseat. Avoid allowing your Rottweiler to ride in the front seat with you, even when he is in his travel harness and buckled in. A deployed air bag could kill or seriously injure him.

Dog/Baby Gates

Whether you're bringing home a puppy or a seasoned adult, you don't want to give the new Rottweiler the opportunity to run through the house unsupervised. A good investment is a set of dog or baby gates that can be moved from room to room to keep your Rottweiler with you and supervised. When your Rottweiler can be trusted to be left alone in your home, you may still want to use these gates to keep him in certain areas.

Identification

Many dogs are lost every year and never rejoined with their families because they lack identification.

If you can't fit a crate in your car, make sure you purchase a harness that attaches to the seatbelt and is designed specifically for dogs riding in cars.

Dogs that are loose can travel incredible distances relatively quickly. For this reason alone, it is wise to have dog tags ready for your new Rottweiler when you pick him up, and then add a permanent form of identification at a later date.

Tags: The advantages to dog tags are that they are a cheap, quick way to immediately identify your dog. They also serve another less obvious purpose: Strangers are much more likely to approach a stray dog *with* tags than they would a stray with *no* tags. The disadvantage to tags is that they can fall or pull off. Once the tag is off, so is the means of identification.

Tattoos: Dogs are generally tattooed on the inner thigh but can also be tattooed on the inside of the earflap. The number is registered with a national registry that maintains ownership and contact information on the dog. A drawback to this system is that dogs must be mature to be tattooed on the thigh. If tattooed as a puppy, the tattoo may stretch and distort as the puppy grows, and become unrecognizable. Also, not everyone will check for a tattoo or know how to find the registry.

Microchips: Microchips are about the size of a grain of rice and are implanted with a needle under the skin and between the shoulder blades. The process does not require anesthesia, and seems to create only temporary discomfort. The microchip is permanent. A scanner reads the information from the microchip, at which time the national registry for the chip can be contacted and the owner reunited with the dog.

Drawbacks to this system include that not all scanners can read the different types of microchips, and most people would never know a dog had a microchip unless the dog's tag indicated this—and then you'd have the information you needed anyway—or the dog wound up at a shelter that routinely scans for microchips.

Newspapers

If you've been recycling newspapers, get out of the habit and start stockpiling now. Your very own black-and-rust recycler is about to trot into your house. You'll need lots of thick layers of fresh newspapers to line his crate. Though your Rottweiler might enjoy a nice pad in his crate, you're best off delaying this

purchase until later; you'll want to make sure he is house-trained, and that he's not a shredder!

Food and Bowls

If there is one purchase you make before you bring your Rottweiler home, make sure it is your dog's food. And, make sure it is the exact brand of food that your breeder or the breed rescue has been feeding him. The reason for this is simple. Sudden changes of food can cause intestinal distress or diarrhea. If you'd like to change foods later on, you can do so gradually over a period of 10 days (see Changing Foods, page 111).

Bowls for food and water should be metal or ceramic. You might like the nontippable type, which can save on cleanup. Both metal and ceramic bowls can be washed in the dishwasher.

Treats

A sack of nice dog treats or biscuits should always be on hand for training. Don't go overboard on feeding treats, however, since this can upset your Rottweiler's system. Many dog food manufacturers are now making treats and biscuits that have the same protein content as their foods. These are good choices because they are not high in sugars or salts, and since they are similar in content to the dog's food, they shouldn't present too much of a dietary change.

Training with treats: Always make your Rottweiler work for her treats. Never dole them out without requiring him to do *something,* such as a *sit.* It's a great way to establish leadership with your Rottweiler from an early age—and it's a fun way to teach commands. Consider wearing a fanny pack filled with little morsels at home so you can train and treat your Rottweiler intermittently throughout the day. You'll also be able to reward instantly when you catch him doing something good, rather than having to run for a treat.

Toys, Toys, Toys

Your new Rottweiler, whether he is a puppy or an adult, will need an assortment of toys and chews to keep him happy. There are racks and racks of chews and toys available in pet stores. Unfortunately, many or even most are unsuitable for Rottweilers. Toys that should be avoided include:

• Rubber and latex squeekie toys (they'll last only a few minutes, if that)
• Balls or toys that can be swallowed
• Tennis balls (your Rottweiler will tear the skin off and could choke)
• Rawhide or compressed rawhide bones that can be chewed into pieces and swallowed in lumps
• Hooves that can splinter and break into pieces

So what can you give to your Rottweiler? Basically, there are two groups of toys and chews that are suitable for your dog:

1. Those that can be given to your dog only if you are supervising his play or chewing time
2. Those that can be given to your dog when he is by himself or in his crate. These are usually referred to as "busy" toys and chews.

The first set of toys and chews can include those that are entertaining for your Rottweiler but are potentially perishable. In other words, they could pop, break or tear after a lot of use, so they should be used only when you can supervise your Rottweiler's play. Large, tough squeekie balls would fall into this category, as would some of the soft plush toys; hard, baked, or compressed chew bones; and nylon bones—if they are large enough not to be swallowed.

Toys and chews that you could leave your Rottweiler alone with include some of the large rope toys that double as canine floss; the "almost" Indestructible Ball, which is great for outside play; hard plastic treat cubes or balls that release treats as the dog plays with the toy; and large, hard rubber balls and

Rottweilers are notorious for being tough on their toys. Make sure you only purchase toys for your Rottweiler that are safe and virtually indestructible.

saucer-shaped toys that have slots into which you can insert biscuits. These toys are safe, virtually indestructible, and in the case of the treat cubes, balls, and rubber biscuit toys, the dog can work for hours to try to release a few treats.

Antichew Salves and Sprays

Typically if a puppy or adult is going to chew on something, such as a cabinet, table leg, or windowsill, he usually goes for one spot or area to do his chewing. Antichewing salves or sprays are available at pet supply stores and have a bitter taste that repels most dogs. Very determined Rottweilers or those with "no taste" are unaffected, however.

Stain Removers

There are many products that promise to remove urine and feces stains permanently and effectively. Talk with other pet owners to see what they're using that's effective. You might also visit a pet store for ideas, and a carpet store, which usually stocks a variety of cleaning products.

Grooming Equipment

Rottweilers do shed, and black-and-mahogany hairs can be found wafting through the halls and stuck in upholstery just about any time of year. Fall and spring are, of course, the worst. Regular grooming can keep a lot of this shedding in check (see discussions on brushing and bathing, Chapter Ten), so be sure that you're equipped with the right tools from the beginning.

Brushes: You'll want to find a good, sturdy bristle dog grooming brush and a pin brush, which is a brush with pinlike bristles with rounded ends.

Toenail clippers: If you are buying a puppy, you won't need a large, heavy-duty clipper yet and can start off with a medium-size clipper. Or, if you are planning on using a toenail grinder, be sure to get this now so you can acclimate your puppy to the sound and smell (see Electric Grinders, page 104).

Rottweiler-proofing Your Home

While you're gathering up all the essentials you'll need to start your new Rottweiler's life off right, you'll need to make sure that your home and Rottweiler will be safe. The following are a few things to consider when looking around your house for potential dangers.

Electrical cords: If your puppy manages to chew through a cord to a lamp or appliance that is turned on and is plugged into a socket, the jolt could be severe. Additionally, if your puppy manages to chew partially through the cord, the exposed wires become a fire hazard. *Keep electrical cords out of sight and out of reach of your puppy.*

Shoes: Shoes are prime targets for Rottweilers of all ages, and it seems that the more expensive the shoe, the better. If you want to keep the shoes you have, keep them on your feet or put them in the closet *and shut the door.*

Counters: Anything that is left on the counter is within reach of a Rottweiler and is, therefore, fair game. The best ways to keep your Rottweiler away from the counter are to either crate him or keep your counter clear.

Garbage: One of the most frequent complaints among dog owners is that their dogs raid the garbage and strew it around the house. The simple solution for people with garbage bandits is this: Keep your garbage locked up. Put it behind cabinet doors or store it in the garage.

Knickknacks: Once your Rottweiler is mature, his agility and grace may actually surprise you, but until this time, anything breakable or valuable should be stowed out of reach of your Rottweiler.

Furniture: If you plan to allow your Rottweiler up on certain chairs or sofas (and this should *only* be when you've invited him to do this), you may want to consider putting a cover or blanket over the chair. The Rottweiler's dark hairs seem to gravitate to light-colored upholstery and, regardless of upholstery color, the hairs stick in the fabric like barbed hooks. A cover or blanket can make cleaning as simple as washing the blanket every week.

Household products: Many household cleaners and other products are toxic to dogs, sometimes in very small quantities. Make sure toilet cleaners and fresheners are behind closed doors, as well as any supplies you use for cleaning. Roach motels, pesticides, and rodenticides should not used in any place where your Rottweiler could possibly get into them. Antifreeze, though usually stored in the garage, should *never* be available to your Rottweiler. Even a tiny puddle on the garage floor could be lethal to a curious puppy.

Rottweiler-proofing Your Yard

One glance at your backyard and you might think everything looks fine and should be a safe haven for your new Rottweiler. If you really look closely, however, you might find that you can make some improvements.

Fences

A fence is a must for Rottweiler ownership. You cannot let your Rottweiler run loose, nor would you want him to. There are many kinds of fences being used to enclose backyards, including chain link, wooden privacy fences, and buried electric fence systems—all with their advantages and drawbacks. (If you live in a neighborhood with a homeowner's association, be aware that you may not have a choice as to what kind of fencing you can use.) Ideally, whether the fence is wood or chain link, it should be at least 6 feet (1.8 m) tall.

Chain link: These fences provide your Rottweiler with an opportunity

Liability on a Chain

Keeping a dog on a chain in the yard is an unacceptable way to keep any dog, much less a Rottweiler. Chaining a dog in a yard is a certain way to create a fearful or overly defensive dog, no matter how wonderful a temperament the dog had to begin with.

When the chained dog has developed an attitude toward other animals, dogs, and/or people, it then becomes a liability. Statistically, approximately one-third of all dog bites occur when a person enters a chained dog's territory.

to watch everything that is going on both in and out of his territory. Rottweilers love to see what is going on. Drawbacks to chain link fences are that mean-spirited people may tease your dog from the other side. Also,

At first glance your yard may look safe for your puppy, but be sure to check for poisonous plants, loose boards in the fence, and other hazards.

some Rottweilers can figure out how to climb the chain link to get out.

Wooden privacy fence: The slick, smooth surface of this fence makes it much more difficult to climb. A drawback is that your Rottweiler will not be able to see what is going on outside the fence, but he will be able to hear what is going on, which could be frustrating to him. A solution to this problem can be to cut knotholes at approximately "eye" height so that your Rottweiler can peek out and at least see what is making a noise or sound.

Buried electric fence system: With this system, the dog wears a collar that, when he nears the buried electric fence, begins to buzz with a warning. If the dog gets too close to the fence line, the collar will give him an electric zap. These fences can be very helpful when paired with another fencing system, such as a privacy or chain link fence, that the dog is attempting to escape from.

However, an electric fence system by itself is not advised for a Rottweiler for three reasons:

1. The fence works only when the power is on. During an electrical storm when your power is knocked out, so is your fence

2. Some Rottweilers will be so focused on something outside of the fence that they will suffer through the shock.

3. The electric fence will keep your Rottweiler in, but it will not keep other animals and children out. With the natural territorial characteristics of this breed, having a loose dog in

A good, sturdy fence is essential for your backyard and the security of your Rottweiler.

a fenceless yard is asking for an accident.

Poisonous Plants

Many plants are toxic to dogs, so you'll want to take a close look at what is growing in your backyard, as well as what types of houseplants you have in the home.

Reactions to poisonous plants can include gastrointestinal upset, and irritation or swelling of the mouth and throat. Some plants affect heart rhythm, other plants can cause hallucinations.

If you can't remove the plant, (perhaps you have a beautiful, mature cherry tree, which is extremely toxic), you will want to think of a way to keep your dog from coming in contact with the toxic plant. For additional information on which plants are toxic in your area, consult with your veterinarian.

Pools

If you have a pool in your backyard, you will need to take the same precautions with your Rottweiler as you would with a young child. Make sure your dog knows how to swim and that he knows how to get out of the pool. If your Rottweiler doesn't know where the steps are to the pool, there could be tragic consequences. If you can't supervise, make sure your pool is fenced so that your dog doesn't have access to the pool when you're not present.

Prepare Your Family

Your home and yard are safe and ready for the new dog, but is your family ready? If you have children, you will want to go over the rules of good dog ownership with them (see rules for kids and dogs, page 80).

You'll also need to discuss with your family who will be responsible for training the dog and for supervising his care. All family members should contribute to the dog's care, but someone must be ultimately responsible, and this should be one of the parents.

The ground rules for what will be allowed and what will not be allowed regarding the dog should also be discussed before the dog comes home. If you don't want the dog to be able to sit on the couch, or perhaps the formal dining room is off limits, then everyone must agree to keep these rules. If one family member is lenient with the dog, the Rottweiler will take this inch and run with it.

Kids and Chores

How old should a child be before he or she can take responsibility for caring for a dog? It really depends on the child. As one child psychologist pointed out, if the child still needs to be reminded to brush his teeth every morning and every night, then expecting this child to remember on his own to feed the dog every morning and every night is beyond reason.

For most children under the age of 13, active parental involvement is required to make sure that the child takes care of the dog chores and does them adequately. Young children can be quite capable of helping with dog chores if they work as a "team" with a parent. Older teenagers can be capable of caring for a puppy or adult dog, but often their schedules are so hectic that a parent may still need to be involved to make sure that the necessary dog chores are completed.

The bottom line is that the parent is ultimately responsible for the care of the dog. When children are involved in the dog's care, the parent must oversee all activities and make sure that everything is accomplished correctly. If you, as a parent, aren't ready to take the full responsibility of the dog's care, then you should consider waiting until a later date to acquire a dog.

Take Time Off

One important consideration you'll need to make is to take time off to spend with him. The first week is usually the most difficult as far as lack of sleep for the new owner, for instance, frequent walks during the night, howling, and crying, and you might consider staying at home during this week. You'll get a chance to catch up a little on your sleep, and your Rottweiler will adjust more quickly to your home and lifestyle if you initially spend a lot of time with him.

Chapter Eight
Welcome Home

Welcoming home a new Rottweiler puppy or a rescued adult Rottweiler is an exciting time. It is also an exhausting time. Both puppy and adult will be looking to their new owners for nurturing, comfort, and guidance. This is an important responsibility that should not be taken lightly, but it is also a responsibility that if handled correctly, will be rewarded beyond words by your Rottweiler. And, even though the initial days and maybe weeks can be demanding, especially if you are dealing with a rambunctious puppy, these times are also fun.

Bringing Home Your New Puppy

If you've done your homework and thoroughly prepared for your new puppy, you will have all the supplies you need and already will have made an appointment with your veterinarian (see Chapter Seven). Now it is time to pick up your Rottweiler puppy and bring her home.

• In the excitement of going to the breeder, make sure you remember to pack a few things in your car: a collar with dog tags, a leash, and a crate lined with a thick layer of newspapers. You may also want to bring a bottle of water and a water bowl if you are traveling any longer than an hour in the car. Since your puppy will miss her littermates and mother for the first several nights, be sure to ask the breeder to allow the mother to lie on a towel or small blanket (you can drop the item off in advance), so that you use this scented article to help comfort your puppy.

• Don't forget to bring a roll of paper towels and a few extra newspapers. If your puppy hasn't traveled much in the car, there's a good chance she might get carsick along the way. If she does, you'll want to clean her up immediately and replace the papers in her crate so she's comfortable for the rest of the ride.

• On the way home, you can expect your Rottweiler to pant, cry, and whine a bit, even with the scented article. This is her first time away from her littermates and possibly her mother, too, so she will naturally miss them. Everything is new for her, as well. Your car won't smell like the breeder's car and she has met you

The moment you bring your puppy home, she is totally dependent on you for nurturing and guidance.

that puppies need rest, too. Make sure she knows where her crate is and keep the door open so she can curl up in there when she wants to.

• Don't forget to keep to her feeding schedule. She will be eating three times a day and the meals need to be spaced roughly six hours apart—for instance, 6:00 A.M., 12:00 P.M., 6:00 P.M. Fresh water should be available to her at all times, but to help with house-training, you can pick up her water about two hours before you plan to call it a night.

• When you're ready to go to sleep, make sure you take your Rottweiler pup out one last time to relieve herself. Then, move the crate up to your bedroom so she can see you, put clean newspapers in the bottom, and fluff up the scented article you have for her to sleep with. Some owners like to put a clock in a thick sock so that the puppy can hear the ticking sound. Others like to wrap a hot water bottle in a towel to provide the puppy the warmth she is used to when she slept in a puppy pile with her siblings. You can give her a safe chew or toy (see Toys, Toys, Toys, page 75), put her in the crate, shut the door, and turn off the light.

But, don't be too set on sleeping . . .

only once or twice before now, so she really doesn't know you yet. Empathize with her anxiety, but also know that she will bond to you quickly and it will be only a matter of time before she leaves thoughts of her siblings well behind her.

• When you bring her home, make sure to allow her to relieve herself immediately upon coming out of her crate. Lead her to a place that is suitable and allow her to sniff around until she picks a spot. Bring her crate in from the car and place it in the room where you will want her to be during the day. If she hasn't eliminated outside, you may want to play with her in the backyard until she *has* relieved herself. The fewer times she has an accident inside, the faster her house-training will go (see House-training 101, page 96).

• Though you may be tempted to play all day with her, keep in mind

The First Night

If you haven't raised a puppy in a while, or if you've never raised a puppy, you'll quickly remember, or find out, just how much noise an eight-week-old puppy in a crate can make. You also will be amazed at the range of sounds that can emanate from a Rottweiler puppy: crying, whining, howling, yodeling, barking, as well as sounds that literally defy description!

Sleeping on Your Bed

If your puppy is not letting you get any sleep, you might be tempted to let her out of her crate and put her in bed. Resist the urge. Unless you sleep *very* lightly and are guaranteed to wake up when your Rottweiler puppy so much as moves or whispers a whimper, you are likely to wake up to a soiled bed or a missing Rottweiler puppy. And if she's not on the bed, you know you'll be in for an unpleasant surprise . . .

Allowing a dog to sleep in the bed can invite future dominance problems, too. Dogs that are allowed to sleep in bed with their masters—regardless of breed—often interpret this to mean that they have an equal or even greater status than the owner. (Not good.) Additionally, it may be easy to pick up a puppy off the bed *now* when you want her off, but it is far more difficult to tell a full-grown Rottweiler to get off the bed when she doesn't want to.

However, if you do choose to allow your Rottweiler in bed with you, you must teach and enforce the *off* command. This can be done with a young dog by gently taking her by the collar and saying, *"Off"* every time you coax her off a chair or the bed. Reward her good behavior with a treat, and practice this command! The *"off"* command will come in handy as your Rottweiler grows.

Sleepless Nights

Though the horrendous noises coming from your puppy are a natural response to her being separated from her fellow puppies and mother, they are virtually impossible to sleep through. What can you do? Some owners grin and bear it, knowing that the next night will be better, as will the next and the next until finally, the puppy will sleep quietly—until she has to relieve herself.

Rather than gutting out the first several sleepless nights, some owners will meet the puppy halfway.

The treatment a puppy receives in the home will have a major impact on what she will be like as an adult.

They'll pull up a sleeping bag and pillow next to the puppy and slip a finger or two into the crate for the puppy to cuddle up next to. This can work very well with some pups, as long as the owner doesn't mind sleeping on a hard floor for a few nights. Within a night or two the owner should be able to move back into his or her bed, and keep the crate nearby so the puppy can see her owner.

Figuring out when the puppy is agitated about being left alone and when she really has to relieve herself can be difficult to discern the first few nights. A young puppy will need to be walked sometime in the middle of the night if she is to avoid soiling her crate. Once she has settled into the routine of being crated at night better, when she cries or whines you will know it is because she has an urgent urge.

The First Weeks

Once you have a good routine going and your Rottweiler is settling in, it is time to begin working on your puppy's training (see The Basics of a Well-behaved Rottweiler, pages 136–147), and her socialization skills.

Socializing Skills Begin Now

One of the most critical socialization periods for a puppy begins while the puppy is with her mother and littermates, and ends roughly around 12 weeks. What experiences a puppy is exposed to in her first four weeks in her new home, therefore, are essential to her development as a well-socialized dog. This socialization includes both dogs and people.

Dogs: Rottweilers are generally not dog aggressive. Owners of well-socialized Rottweilers note that Rottweilers are generally delightful to take to dog parks and play very well with dogs of all sizes.

However, don't take for granted that your Rottweiler will be dog friendly. Frightening experiences with adult dogs as a puppy or no experiences with adult dogs can make a Rottweiler puppy develop into a dog-aggressive canine.

To start your Rottweiler off on the right paw, begin by introducing her to friendly, fully vaccinated, and healthy dogs on neutral territory. Once your puppy is fully vaccinated herself, she can begin attending puppy kindergarten or preschool classes and will have the opportunity to meet and play with lots of other puppies.

People: If your Rottweiler's experiences with people are always positive as she grows up, she will develop a good attitude toward people that will extend into adulthood. Take advantage of this and make sure to take your puppy with you on walks and introduce her to as many types of people as possible.

People that you particularly want to introduce your Rottweiler to include delivery people, your postal person, children, and people of all races and ages, if possible. As your

Rottweiler ages, she may become more territorial and protective of you and your home. Your goal is to make sure that outside of the home in "neutral" territory, your dog is comfortable with people. In her own territory, you want her to be able to immediately recognize friends from foes by the tone of your voice and your mannerisms.

A Friend Is a Treat Away

A great way to introduce your Rottweiler puppy to new people is to put her in a *sit* (see Sit, page 140). With your puppy by your side and in her *sit,* ask the "stranger" to reward your puppy with a treat, which you have in your pocket, of course. Lavish your puppy with praise and pats, and if the person is willing, have him or her pat your puppy, too. Soon, your Rottweiler will associate an extended hand with something very good.

If your Rottweiler is a bit wary or fearful and appears uncomfortable when meeting new people, it is very important to keep working with her. A fearful Rottweiler puppy will grow into a fearful adult, which is potentially a dangerous animal.

To work with the timid puppy, make sure she stays in her *sit,* but don't allow the stranger too close to your dog. Keep the person at a comfortable distance from your puppy and have him or her toss the puppy a treat. To make the puppy even more at ease with the stranger, see if the person will be willing to sit down so he or she does not appear

Socializing skills begin with a puppy and continue through a dog's adult life.

so threatening. (You may need to call on your friends for this type of cooperation.)

Owners of puppies that growl or snarl aggressively toward people should seek qualified, expert help. If aggression is recognized in puppies, animal behaviorists say that some cases can be corrected and many others can be remodeled so that the dog is controllable and does not pose a threat.

Keep in mind that the leash you are holding is like a telegraph line to your puppy. Rottweilers are uncanny with their ability to read their owners' minds and emotions. If you are nervous that your Rottweiler might not behave when greeting a stranger, your Rottweiler will pick up on the fact that you are nervous, but she won't have any idea why you are nervous. The fact that you are anxious about something is all it will take for many Rottweilers to respond with aggression to protect you! So, be sure that you do not accidently send your puppy the wrong message, or a mixed one.

Habituating the Puppy

Rottweilers, even as puppies, are fairly confident dogs. For the most part, they will take everything they see with few qualms. Even those experiences that may initially startle them, such as the first time you turn on the garbage disposal, will usually be ignored the second time they hear them. The following is a list of everyday activities, sights, or sounds that you need to take special care with to make sure your Rottweiler grows up well adjusted.

Car Travel

Puppies will often get carsick, generally because they are nervous about traveling in the car. The worst thing you can do if this is the case with your puppy is to not travel by car. What you want to do is travel more frequently with your puppy, but perhaps keeping the trips very short. Always make the trips fun; you don't want your puppy to associate car travel with a trip to the veterinarian. Try to visit parks and play.

Or drive to a pleasant area to walk your puppy. Eventually, even the travel-sick puppy will calm down and/or outgrow her carsickness.

Note: Acclimating your puppy to car travel and actually taking her on regular and frequent car rides serves another important purpose. Some Rottweilers can be so protective of their families and homes that they literally need to be crated every time someone comes to the door. Rottweiler experts seem to think the breed's natural protectiveness can escalate to this level if the puppy is not taken out of the home on a regular basis.

When you go on a walk or take a ride in a car to a park, you are leaving "home" and entering neutral territory. This simple exercise seems to help many Rottweilers keep their lives and jobs in perspective. They will still protect you from "bad" guys either in your home or out in neutral territory, but the dogs that are constantly exposed to new people and positive experiences outside of the home seem to be better balanced at home.

Grooming

Toenails: You may not need to trim your puppy's toenails for weeks after you've brought her home, but if you don't practice toenail trimming, or using a toenail grinder, you might have a significant struggle on your hands. Practice touching a few toenails with the clipper or grinder each day. Praise and reward your dog for calmness. Eventually, you'll be able to work on a paw at a time.

Brushing: Brushing should also be practiced regularly, even if your puppy doesn't need it. If you choose to use a vacuum attachment for pets, you'll need to begin this procedure with your puppy at a young age, too.

Bathing

Your Rottweiler puppy may not need a bath for months if you keep her clean and well brushed; however, if you don't practice bathtime while your puppy is small and willing, convincing an adolescent Rottweiler to hop into the tub for a scrub may be virtually impossible.

For more on grooming, see Chapter Ten.

Working with Resource Guarding

A very important skill to teach your puppy at a young age is that she must give you whatever she has in her mouth when you ask for it. This can be trained at an early age by giving the command *"Out,"* and offering a yummy treat in exchange for the toy. Be sure to give the command when you know she will be willing to give up her toy; in other words, set her up for success. After you have given her the treat, you can return the toy to her.

This exercise should also be practiced with food bowls. Offer your puppy a yummy treat for allowing you to take away her bowl. Then return the bowl to her. This simple exercise will prevent any squabbles when she is older.

If your Rottweiler refuses the treat swap and growls, snarls, or even snaps at you, giving up is not the answer; this problem will only get worse. However, the situation may be more than you can handle safely. Be sure to consult an experienced trainer, certified animal behaviorist, or veterinary animal behaviorist for guidance on how to work through this problem. An experienced Rottweiler breeder can also be of enormous help. Remember: It's much easier to work out this problem with a smaller puppy that poses no real danger than a mature Rottweiler that has been allowed to get away with this behavior for months or even years.

Rehoming the Rescued Rottweiler

Bringing home a rescued Rottweiler in many ways is similar to bringing home a puppy, except that the adult dog is obviously quite a bit bigger and fully developed. If you think you will escape the first night of howling and crying, you might be surprised instead with how much noise a 100+ pounds (45+ kgs) of dog can make in a crate. As a general rule, most adult dogs settle in a bit faster than puppies, and if they've relieved themselves before to retiring for the night, they should be able to go through the night without any accidents.

Each rescued Rottweiler, of course, will be different in her needs and requirements to successfully adjust her to her new home. The breed rescue you are working with will be able to give you good suggestions on what types of things your Rottweiler will need work on to help her get settled in. Generally, most dogs will need to accept you as their leader, as well as receive habituation and socialization training.

If your Rottweiler doesn't want to give up a toy, there's no way you're going to get it! Teach the "out" command at an early age and practice it with food rewards.

Bonding

Adult dogs are capable of forming very deep bonds with their new owners.

If the Rottweiler has come from a dire situation with little affection or care, often she will be looking for someone. As incredible as this seems, rescue workers say it happens all the time. Once given the care, leadership, and attention the dog craves, she quickly accepts the new owner and bonds deeply with him or her. The same is true of adult Rottweilers that have experienced good homes but for whatever reason (perhaps the death of the owner) are relinquished. Given time and patience, the dog will bond and become very attached.

One of the fastest ways to cement the new bond is to begin obedience training. Even if the dog knows her commands, when a new owner begins giving her the commands, she recognizes her position as "second in command." The more the owner and dog work together, the faster and deeper the bond that forms. These dogs love to work and they are exceptionally bright. Training gives them the job they are seeking.

Habituation Training

Many of the rescue dogs coming through breed rescues and shelters have limited experiences in the home. If the dog possesses the confident temperament of the breed, usually she takes new experiences, such as steps, slick floors, the

Rottweiler puppies should be socialized with other puppies and older dogs so that they will continue to not be dog-aggressive as adults.

sound of the dishwasher or garbage disposal, and toilets flushing, in stride. She may be inquisitive or startled at first, but once she figures out that these stimuli pose no threat to her or her new family, she will act as if she grew up in a home.

Other dogs, those, in particular, that are perhaps a bit mistrustful at first, may need more exposure to home life before they begin to feel comfortable with the sights and sounds that we accept as being normal. If your dog expresses surprise

Car Travel for Adult Rottweilers

Being able to take your adult Rottweiler in the car is important. You'll need to take her to the veterinarian and to training classes, and you'll also want to be able to take her almost anywhere else you *can* take her. In order to do this, you'll need to work with her so that she is not afraid of traveling in a car. The following are some steps you can take to help your adult Rottweiler overcome her trepidations toward travel.

1. Make sure she is crate trained. If your Rottweiler feels at home in her crate, allowing her to ride in the car (a scary thing) in her crate (a comforting thing) will help her feel safer and she will be less apprehensive.

2. Start off slowly. If she is very afraid of the car, begin by trying to get her close to the car by tossing treats near the car while she is on a leash and the engine is off. If you can convince her to climb into the car, begin feeding her in her crate in the car.

3. Progress in baby steps. Once you've got her comfortable in the car with the engine off, get her in her crate and turn the engine on for just a brief time, then turn it off and take her out.

4. Roll down the driveway. After your Rottweiler is comfortable with getting in and out of the car, and having the engine turned on and running for a few minutes, next try

rolling down the driveway. If this goes well, drive back up the driveway, and take out the dog. (Your neighbors will think you are absolutely crazy at this point, but don't worry—you're almost there with your dog!)

5. Go around the block. Take a short drive—around the block is fine, or if you have a park where you can walk your dog or play ball with her, then stop there. You want to associate good things with car rides.

6. Battling sickness. If an adult dog gets ill when she travels, you can help her by making sure she doesn't eat a full meal before traveling, keeping the air circulating well in her crated area, and making sure that she is in a crate in which she can easily see out. Many times, carsickness is caused by anxiety. As your dog travels more often, this should ease. Sometimes, however, the carsickness is truly a form of motion sickness or may be related to some other condition. If, after working with your dog for several weeks or even months, she doesn't seem to be improving or if she gets *really* ill from traveling, consult your veterinarian. There are medications available to help anxiety and motion sickness. If another condition is causing the sickness, your veterinarian will be the person to diagnose this.

or fear toward a new sound or sight in the home, ignore the response. If you try to comfort your dog with pats and "It's O.K., Baby," you will inadvertently be reinforcing the wrong behavior. Your Rottweiler doesn't see it as comfort; she sees your praise as good words for a job well done. In other words, your Rottweiler will think she displayed an appropriate response (fearfulness) to the sight or sound and will repeat this response the next time she is exposed to the stimuli.

If you catch your dog not responding to a sight or sound that she had previously been frightened or wary of, *then* you can praise her.

Socialization Skills

Generally, rescued Rottweilers will not have had the extensive socialization training that a well-raised puppy will have had. This means that the rescued Rottweiler may be more wary of strangers that normal. If this is the case, you will need to carefully work on your rescued Rottweiler's behavior toward new people. Never compromise the safety of anyone while working on socialization skills. If your Rottweiler appears aggressive toward people, this is extremely dangerous and requires the help of a certified animal behaviorist or a veterinary animal behaviorist.

If your Rottweiler wants to be friendly with people but is unsure of herself, then the same training exercise that is used for puppies (see A

Friend Is a Treat Away, page 85) can be used with the adult dog. You'll need to make sure your Rottweiler is very good with her *sit* command first, however.

In general, you'll need to take things much slower with the rescued adult.
• Don't overwhelm her.
• Take little steps and expect to take a step backward now and then.
• Make sure you don't push her training too fast; start off at her pace. She may progress slowly at first, but as she gains trust in you, you will see her begin to blossom in other areas, too.

Your Rottweiler's dream is to work beside you. Give her this opportunity and she will flourish.

Chapter Nine

Crate Training and House-training

Chewed-up shoes. Accidents on the new carpet. A broken screen door. A hole in the drywall. A monster pit in the backyard. Rottweilers can be very destructive when left alone. Without any guidance or direction, most Rottweilers will find something to do to entertain themselves. Unfortunately, what the Rottweiler usually chooses is an activity that is not constructive.

Much of this destructive behavior can be prevented by giving your Rottweiler enough exercise, attention, and training. (Remember: The Rottweiler wants to have a job!) In addition to providing activities for your Rottweiler, a crate can be a valuable tool in preventing destructive and unwanted behaviors.

What Is Crate Training?

Crate training is basically the use of a crate to safely confine a dog in an area where he can't harm anything or injure himself. The crate is not used as punishment, but rather a safe haven for your dog when you can't watch his every move. Crating is not intended to replace exercise, attention, and training; your Rottweiler needs to get outside and move. He also needs extensive mental stimulation, but for those times when you absolutely can't watch him, and especially during house-training, the crate is an important tool for the Rottweiler owner.

Selecting the Crate

Type

Choosing the right type of crate and sizing it correctly for your Rottweiler is important to the success of crate training. There are many types of crates available on the market today: metal or wire; hard-shell plastic; and lightweight mesh.

Metal: The metal or wire crates are typically fairly heavy, but a collapsible crate can be broken down and stored very easily. Metal crates have pans that can be taken out to be washed, which makes cleaning up after a puppy very easy. Metal crates also provide your Rottweiler a 360-degree view of his world—

something a Rottweiler greatly appreciates. Air circulation is also very good with these crates, which could be a consideration if your SUV or wagon doesn't have very good air flow in the cargo area.

Plastic: Hard-shell plastic crates come in two pieces: a top and a bottom. They are more difficult to clean up during house-training (feces and urine seem to work their way into every crack and fissure), and they don't provide your Rottweiler a good view of his world. Some plastic carriers are approved for air travel. The hard-shell plastic crates are lighter to carry than metal crates, but since they break into only two pieces, they tend to take up more room when storing. There is also no way to put a divider in a plastic crate to downsize it for a young puppy. Perhaps someone will come up with a design soon!

Tent: The third type of crate is made of fabric, lightweight mesh, and PVC tubing. It is reminiscent of a very light tent. These crates fold down into virtually nothing, and are extremely easy to break down and store or carry. They are not recommended for new puppies or dogs, however, for the following reasons:

1. A Rottweiler with even half a mind to get out of his crate can shred the tent in a matter of seconds.

2. Even a little puppy can throw his body against the sides and make the crate hop or move to where he'd like to go. (And Rottweiler puppies have done this!)

He may behave perfectly when you're around, but watch out! Every Rottweiler has the ability to be destructive when left alone.

3. The crate is not safe for any kind of travel, air or car; however, it is a breezy light crate that could be used with a dog that is very trustworthy, particularly when traveling. With this crate, you could travel with the dog in his regular metal or plastic crate, then set up this tent in the hotel room—but, again, it's not for crate training or house-training!

Sizing a Crate

If you are purchasing a crate for an adult dog, your job is easy. You need to find a crate in which your dog can stand without crouching, turn completely around, and lie down comfortably. Most Rottweilers will require a large crate, with some very large Rottweilers needing an extra-large. A very small Rottweiler might fit a medium crate, but he would have to be quite small.

If you are sizing a crate for a puppy, you need to use a crate that fits the above criteria, and that is not too big for your puppy. Using a "just right"-sized crate for a puppy helps greatly with house-training. If you put a puppy in a crate that has just enough room for him, he will let you know when he has to relieve himself and will try to hold until you can get to him. If, on the other hand, you put him in a crate that has lots of room in it, he will be able to relieve himself in a corner and sleep comfortably away from the mess in another corner.

Rottweiler puppy owners are therefore faced with three options.

1. They can buy a crate that is slightly larger than the puppy's needs and plan on buying another larger crate once the puppy is fairly reliable about alerting his owners to his needs and not soiling his current crate (at roughly around four to five months).

2. To save money, if the owner happens to know someone with a small or medium-sized crate, he or she could borrow this until the puppy is ready to move up to a full-size crate.

3. The Rottweiler owner could look into purchasing a wire or metal crate that has a divider. The divider can be used to partition a large crate and make a comfortable, smaller area of the young puppy. As the puppy grows, the divider can be moved.

Making the Crate Comfortable

For cost, ease of use, and absorbency, you can't beat newspapers for bedding in a crate. Accidents are easily cleaned up by pulling the sheets out. Many manufacturers make comfortable padding and even beds that can be inserted in the crates, but it is not a good idea to spend money on these items until the Rottweiler is house-trained. A Rottweiler that likes to shred or "fluff' items may also not be a candidate for a comfortable crate bed, unless you're willing to buy a new bed every time the old one is destroyed.

For shredders and fluffers, you might consider using old towels or small, worn blankets. These can be easily washed, and if you've purchased them at a yard sale, you won't be so upset when the item is ripped apart. Do, however, avoid using carpet scraps, as busy puppies and dogs can work the fibers loose and these could present choking hazards.

Acclimating the Rottweiler to the Crate

Many breeds of dogs see the crate as a den, or a protective area in which they can curl up and get away from it all. As a self-confident breed, the Rottweiler tends to take a more independent approach. He'll go in his crate if you ask him to, but he most likely will not seek his crate out. He'd much rather be in the middle of things and, most important, by your side.

Puppies, if put in their crates on a regular basis for short periods of time, will quickly grow to accept their crate. Again, it may not be their favorite place to go, but they will willingly obey you. Adults that have never had any crating growing up may be a little more difficult to get to crate willingly. (And there isn't any way you're going to push a 140-pound [64-kg] male into his crate!)

• To acclimate the dog to his crate, begin by placing the crate in a busy area and leave the door open.

• Toss a few treats in the crate to entice the Rottweiler to go in and out. Don't pounce on him and shut the door the moment he steps in. Wait until you see that he's comfortable going in and out.

• Toss a few more treats in the crate and tell him cheerfully, *"In your kennel!"* When he goes into the crate, praise him, give him a particularly good chew bone, and shut the door.

• Stay within his sight so he doesn't panic, and talk to him. If he howls or barks, don't reward him with comfort. Ignore him.

• After a little time in the crate, you can let him out again. Try to be careful not to let him out when he's barking or whining; this will teach him that carrying on will get him out of his crate.

• Gradually increase the times he stays in his crate and move from room to room so he can't see you. Eventually, leave the house for a few minutes, than a half hour, then a couple of hours.

• Always give your Rottweiler something to do while he's in the crate, such as a really good chew or toy, and reward him each time with a treat or dog cookie immediately upon entering the crate.

Using the Crate

When do you use the crate? Whenever you can't safely confine your Rottweiler or when you can't keep your eyes on him. Crate time should be judicious, however, and not used whenever you don't *want* to keep your eyes on your puppy. There's a difference! In general, your Rottweiler shouldn't be confined for more than ten hours a day *with appropriate breaks.* The longest stretch, if you use the crate during the day, should not exceed three to four hours. Young puppies will need to be let out every two to three hours. If you supervise your puppy during the day and use the crate only at night, he will still need a break during the night to relieve himself.

Adult Rottweilers may be able to stay in their crates for up to six hours or perhaps even a full day, but this should not be without a break. If you work during the day, take off time at lunchtime to walk and play with your dog. He will need it. (It's a good stress buster for you, too.) If you can't take off from work, you might consider hiring someone you trust to walk your dog.

The goal with crate training is to eventually be able to allow the dog more freedom when you are home, and even sometimes when you aren't at home. A dog that is very destructive, suffers from separation anxiety, or that is a little too protective of his home, may still need the crate even as an adult in order to provide him a safe haven.

House-training 101

House-training the Rottweiler is often quite easy if the owner is consistent and uses only positive reinforcement. The key is to set the puppy or dog up for success and limit his chances of failing. The fewer times the Rottweiler fails—that is, soils his crate or eliminates in an inappropriate place in the home— the faster he learns and the less likely he will fail in the future.

Just one accident, particularly if it is in the home and not in the dog's crate, can severely hamper house-training efforts. No matter how well you think you've cleaned up a spot, your Rottweiler will still know that there is a "spot" there. If that odor is left anywhere in the home, it is an invitation to repeat the elimination.

Limiting access: To limit accidents, it is crucial not to expand the puppy or dog's access to the house until he can be trusted in spaces that are easily cleaned. For example, if the crate is kept in the kitchen—a room that usually has a floor that can be scrubbed and is less likely to absorb or retain odor— baby gates can be used to block off this room and allow the Rottweiler access to this room under supervision. When the Rottweiler can live and play in this area and regularly relieves himself outside, then his world can be expanded slowly, room by room.

Knowing the signs: Another critical factor in house-training is recognizing when a puppy or adult needs to relieve himself, and what the signs of an imminent emergency are. Dogs of all ages have to relieve themselves *immediately* upon waking up in the morning, after or during hard play sessions, when they are excited, and within a half hour after eating. Anytime you put your Rottweiler in his crate, you should offer him the opportunity to relieve himself both prior to entering the crate, and immediately upon leaving the crate.

Signs of having to "go," include sniffing and circling. Young puppies may also try to run behind furniture to find an out-of-the-way spot. If you see your Rottweiler acting as if he might have to relieve himself—even if he has just done so moments earlier—take him out.

Scheduling

Sticking to a strict schedule with meals planned at regular times and walks or opportunities for the dog to eliminate first thing in the morning, after eating, midday, and just before retiring for the night, will help house-training immensely. As your dog settles into his schedule, you'll know his routine pretty well and can adjust your schedule to more closely fit his needs.

Fresh, cold water should be available to your Rottweiler all day to prevent gorging on water, which can wreak havoc with house-training, as well as possibly cause other problems, such as bloat (see page 126). You may, however, choose to pick up your dog's water bowl approximately two hours before his last walk of the evening, provided that your dog is not active in any way during these final two hours.

Knowing Limits

Some Rottweilers seem to have incredible "holding" power; whereas, others, on occasion, seem to have peanut bladders. A lot of this has to do with the dog's schedule of feeding and drinking. Age is another factor. Puppies generally can be asked to "hold" for an hour longer than their age in months during the day. For instance, a two-month-old puppy could be asked to wait three hours between walks. Adult dogs may be able to hold for six to eight hours, but many more won't be able to. Regardless whether the adult can or can't go this many hours without relieving himself, perhaps the kinder question is, "Should he be made to wait this long?" It is probably healthiest to be able to provide the adult dog with at least a midday break.

Puppies and adults can be taught to relieve themselves on command, a great convenience when you're in a hurry or in a strange place.

Adding a dog door leading to a fenced backyard is another option.

Rewarding

Just as with training or shaping any other behavior, house-training progresses most quickly with fewest relapses if the puppy or dog is rewarded for relieving himself in the right place. Treats and praise work wonders to cement appropriate behaviors. You can take this one step further and teach your dog a command to relieve himself through rewards.

Teaching the *go now* command: To teach this command, simply give the *go potty* or *go now*

The Rottweiler is an extremely intelligent dog that wants to please you.

command *while your Rottweiler is relieving himself.* Reward him with a treat. Say the *go now* command every time your Rottweiler begins to relieve himself. Through repetition and rewarding, he will quickly pick up on the command.

No Negatives

A common mistake that pet owners make when they are house-training puppies or adults is that they will scold the dog after he has an accident. The only time scolding might work is if you catch the puppy *in the act* of relieving himself. (Physical punishment is never warranted, is counterproductive, and won't be tolerated by your Rottweiler.) If you see your dog in the middle of making a mistake, you can shout *"No!"* or *"Stop!"* Then quickly pick the puppy up or take the dog gently by the collar and hustle him outside. Allow him

to finish his business here, then reward and praise him.

Another owner mistake that is often made in house-training is that the owner calls the dog over to a mistake in order to punish him. What he learns is something quite different from what you had planned. In this instance, your dog learns that if he comes when you call him, he will be punished. Guess who won't come to you the next time you call him? And guess who hasn't learned that relieving himself behind the couch is a bad thing?

If you discover a mess after the fact, *do not punish your dog.* Clean it up thoroughly and try to figure out how *you* messed up. Did you push the envelope on his time limits to "hold?" Have you been irregular with his feeding and exercise schedule? Did you allow him too much freedom in the house too soon? Is he sick? (If a dog has been well house-trained for months or years and suddenly is urinating or defecating inappropriately, have your veterinarian see him immediately.) Once you've figured out your mistake, you can be more careful to set your puppy up for success the next time.

Common House-training Methods

Crate training: As mentioned earlier, the Rottweiler does not want to soil his crate, so he will try hard to keep it clean. If you keep to a schedule of frequent walks, exercise, and regular feeding, the crate can be a great house-training tool.

It is important to remember, however, never to push the limits of your Rottweiler. If you neglect the needs of your Rottweiler and allow your puppy or dog to soil his crate on a regular basis, he could develop "dirty dog syndrome." In this syndrome, a dog that's lived in filth for a long time finally accepts living in his own urine and excrement. Make sure you help your puppy or adult keep his crate clean through short periods in the crate, a feeding schedule, and regular opportunities for exercise and relief.

Confined areas: Another method of house-training involves keeping the puppy or dog confined to a room with a floor that is easy to clean, such as the kitchen, and papering the entire floor. The dog will generally pick a favorite spot to relieve himself. Gradually, the owner can remove papers off the floor, leaving papers only in the dog's favorite spot. The dog is rewarded for relieving himself outside during this whole process. Eventually, all papers can be removed from the training room, and the dog is then praised only when relieving himself outside.

With this method, the same techniques of using a feeding schedule, regular walks and relief periods, and praise are also used. The only drawback to this method is that the owner has to teach the dog where to relieve himself in two steps: First the dog must learn that both "going" on the papers and going outside are O.K., then he must learn not to go inside, but *only* outside.

This method does work but it tends to be a bit slower and more mistakes are often made before the final lesson is learned. Leaving an entire room open to a Rottweiler is also inviting the potential for more damage.

Whichever way you choose to house-train your Rottweiler, remember that even though you own a canine genius, he can control his urges only as nature allows. Be mindful of his needs, and caring and consistent in your training.

Chapter Ten

Grooming and Feeding

There is nothing more beautiful than a healthy Rottweiler. With a thick, glossy black-and-mahogany coat, bright eyes, physical strength, and a vibrance that defies description, a well-cared-for Rottweiler is truly a wonderful sight. Whether she is a show, performance, or companion dog, every Rottweiler that is in good health and that receives the care she so richly deserves, is capable of looking great. All it takes is a little bit of time and some knowledge in basic Rottweiler care.

Brushing

The Rottweiler is a double-coated breed. The outer layer is coarse and straight and somewhat weather resistant. The undercoat is softer and much shorter. In the spring, the Rottweiler will shed her winter coat, which will include part of the extra outer coat that has grown in, particularly if you live in a cold region, and much of the undercoat, which is the dog's natural insulation. Once the days begin to shorten in the fall, your Rottweiler will shed again, though not quite as heavily as before.

During peak shedding seasons, you might be amazed as to the amount of hair that comes out of your dog's coat every day. The stuff will stick to carpets and furniture, waft in clumps in the air, and flit across that floor as you try to chase it down with a broom. Rottweiler hair has even been known to find its way into the refrigerator. You can cut down on the excess hair in your home and on your clothes by regularly brushing your dog.

Technique

A good pin brush is all you will need. The rounded pin bristles of the brush will go deeply into your dog's coat and will help to pull out loose hairs. You can back brush, beginning at your dog's docked tail and working your way through the coat, brushing against the lay of the hair. Once you've gone through the whole coat and loosened up both dead undercoat and outercoat, brush the coat in the right direction.

To catch any additional loose hairs, rub her down with a cloth or use a soft bristle brush.

During non-shedding seasons, your Rottweiler will still lose hairs. When asked when a Rottweiler

Regular brushing will keep loose hairs to a minimum and will lessen the amount of hair wafting around your home.

sheds, a common answer is "When does a Rottweiler *not* shed?" If you give your Rottweiler a quick brush every few days, this should keep the loose hairs pretty well in check. The Rottweiler is not a high-maintenance dog; however, if you want a hairless house, you'll need to work a bit harder on brushing.

Vacuuming . . . The Dog

Vacuuming is not only a good way to rid your furniture and carpets of dog hair and dander, it is also a great way to "brush" your dog. No joke. Many vacuums come with an attachment that is designed for pets. It is a nozzle with rubber teeth. To get rid of hair and dander, you massage the

dog with the nozzle and the vacuum takes care of the rest. It can't be beat during shedding season.

However, you need to practice this with your dog. You won't want to scare a puppy with a loud vacuum, but you can acclimate her first to the sound and then to the feel of the actual nozzle. With practice, your Rottweiler should tolerate grooming with a vacuum.

Adult dogs can be taught to accept this form of brushing, too, if you take it slowly, and if you have taught a good *sit-stay,* or *stand-stay* (see Chapter Thirteen). Don't rush your dog if she is apprehensive and remember to treat and praise good behavior.

Bathing

Fortunately, Rottweilers don't require frequent bathing. In fact, if you regularly brush your Rottweiler, you may need to bathe your dog only once every couple of months, unless she's been excavating in the backyard on a muddy day or found something particularly delightful to roll in. Resist the urge to give your dog a full bath every week; excessive bathing can dry the skin and deplete the dog's coat of natural oils.

When you bathe your Rottweiler, be sure to use a shampoo that is designed for dogs as a dog's skin is different from a human's skin.

You can never miss the vibrant look of a healthy, well-cared-for Rottweiler.

• The water you use to bathe your dog should be warm and comfortable.
• Soak her entirely with clean, warm water before working in the shampoo.
• Be careful not to use too much shampoo because it can be difficult to thoroughly rinse from the dog's undercoat.
• Rinse until you can't feel any soap anywhere, then rinse again just to make sure. If any soap is left in the coat, it can irritate the dog's skin.

If you are washing your Rottweiler in the bathtub, make sure there is a no-slip mat or a thick towel in the bottom to keep your Rottweiler from slipping. If you are washing your dog outside, make sure the weather is warm and comfortable. If it is cool or cold, wash your dog indoors.

After you have thoroughly rinsed the shampoo out, your dog will want to shake (watch out!) and then you can begin drying. If you'd like, you can use a blow dryer to help dry the undercoat. When your Rottweiler is toweled dry, allow her to rest and finish drying off in a warm, dry spot.

Plan Ahead

If it's been awhile since you've washed a dog, here are some extra tips:

1. Wear old clothes.

2. Shut the door to the bathroom. You won't want a full-grown, sudsy Rottweiler to escape her bath and begin running and shaking through your home.

3. Have towels ready. Saying *"Wait"* to your Rottweiler won't keep her from shaking all over you. Make sure you have everything you need within an arm's reach.

4. Wash your dog's bedding before you wash her. There's nothing more frustrating than realizing that the bedding your clean Rottweiler just lay down on smells doggy.

5. Practice. If you have a puppy, practice getting her wet every week so she is used to the bathtub and knows this is a fun activity. Reward good behavior with treats and attention. If you own an adult dog that is not used to baths, begin by getting the dog in the bathtub with no water. Then another day ask her to get in with a little water. Use treats, toys, and praise to encourage her. Work your way up to a full bath.

Nail Trimming

As mentioned in Chapter Eight: Welcome Home, Rottweilers tend to have a "thing" about having their feet touched. They may tolerate having their feet handled but they don't really like it. It is important, however, that your Rottweiler allows you to handle her feet so that her toenails can be trimmed. Toenails that are allowed to grow too long force the toes to splay and eventually can cause damage to the dog's paws. Long toenails also are easily caught in carpet loops and can be broken or pulled out completely.

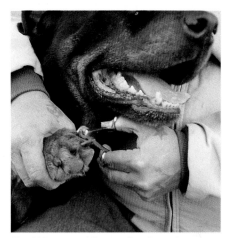

If a 100+ pound Rottweiler doesn't want his toenails clipped, chances are you're not going to be able to clip them. So, begin working with your Rottweiler as a puppy so that he accepts this attention as an adult.

Rottweiler toenails are not easy to trim. Because they are black, you can't tell where the *quick* or nail's blood supply is. Clipping the nail too short is very painful for the dog, and results in a bloody mess. A Rottweiler that has been "quicked" remembers this painful experience and rightfully may not trust you again with her toenails.

Note: There are styptic products available that can be applied to a toenail that has been quicked to help stop the bleeding and avoid infection. They are available at pet supply stores.

So, when you clip, you will want to take off small pieces until you can begin to tell where your dog's quick ends.

If your Rottweiler is very sensitive about her feet, you'll need to start

Ears require only an occasional wipe with a cotton ball to remain healthy, but be sure to practice this with your puppy so that he will tolerate this routine as an adult.

slowly and cut only a nail or two at a time each day. Reward her for good behavior with treats. Eventually, she will get used to the procedure and you may be able to finish all four paws in one sitting.

Electric Grinders

Some breeders prefer to use an electric grinder to trim their dog's nails. The grinder is slower than a traditional nail clipper and the smell and vibration of the grinder can put off some dogs, but the advantages are that you wind up with a very smooth trimmed nail, and if you happen to grind too far, the heat of the grinder will cauterize the cut. Of course, "quicking" the nail will still hurt the Rottweiler, grinder or no grinder.

The grinder takes practice for both the owner and dog. Get your dog used to the sound first before actually grinding a nail. Start off slowly. If your dog tolerates the vibration on her nail, then you can begin grinding a nail at a time.

Eyes and Ears

The healthy Rottweiler's eyes and ears generally do not require much more than a wipe with a damp cotton ball. However, some eye conditions can cause your Rottweiler pain (see Eye Conditions, page 129). If you notice your dog's eyes are bothering her—she's scratching them, rubbing them, or they have a discharge or are swollen or irritated looking—take her to the veterinarian to have them examined. Most eye injuries, diseases, and conditions need to be treated as soon as possible.

Rottweilers are not known to get ear infections more than any other breed; however, pooled water, foreign bodies, such as little twigs or burrs, and allergies can manifest themselves as ear infections.

How do you know if your Rottweiler has an ear infection? Infections smell. If you frequently sniff your healthy Rottweiler's ears, you'll easily be able to smell them if they are infected. Additionally, ear infections create abnormal discharges. Your dog may rub her ears, shake them, or scratch at them. Then again, she might show no signs of pain.

If you suspect an ear infection, take your Rottweiler to your veterinarian immediately. Ear infections that are not treated quickly can quickly progress to a more serious condition.

Dental Care

Eighty-five percent of all dogs over the age of four have periodontal disease. They have bad breath. They have to have teeth pulled. Their gums bleed. They also may be at increased risk for heart disease or other diseases because of the bacteria that is being released into their systems. Dental care is an area in which dog owners can greatly improve the health of their Rottweilers.

Whether you own a puppy or an adult Rottweiler, it is never too late to teach your dog to sit quietly while you brush her teeth. You can begin with a rubber fingerbrush that fits over your finger and has little rubber knobs on it. Most dogs will allow their owners to rub this fingerbrush on the outside of their teeth, especially if it has chicken- or beef-flavored dog toothpaste. Once the dog is used to the fingerbrush, the owner can switch to a dog toothbrush.

Brushing teeth is much like any other skill your dog learns; if you keep the sessions short and positive—and you work on the skill every day—your dog will quickly accept the experience, or at least tolerate it.

Toothpaste for Dogs: When brushing your dog's teeth, be sure to use only toothpaste that is designed for dogs. Some of the ingredients in human toothpaste can be harmful to dogs if swallowed.

Rinsing and Flossing

If your dog has particular problems with her teeth, your veterinarian may recommend a special rinse that can be used in addition to your regular brushing. This rinse is designed for dogs only and is squirted along the gum line to help kill bacteria.

There is no floss for dogs, except for some rope toys that simulate some of the benefits of floss. If you use these rope toys, keep a careful eye on their condition. When the rope toy begins to fray, throw it out and replace it with a new one as a piece of the rope toy potentially could be chewed off and swallowed, causing an obstruction.

Chewing

Dogs with pearly whites are often those that chew a lot. The action of the dog's teeth against a firm chew bone can help to scrape much of the debris away from the gum line. If your dog has a problem with dental disease, you may also want to consult with your veterinarian about what types of food, treats, and toys

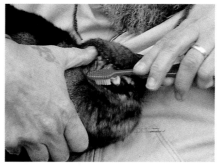

Dental care is far more important to your Rottweiler's overall health than most people realize.

or chews you can use that can help clean your dog's teeth.

Nutrition

Proper nutrition is very important to the overall health of your Rottweiler. If she does not receive the nutrients she needs on a daily basis, she can become malnourished or develop certain diseases. How much you feed your Rottweiler is important, too. Obesity is a significant problem among adult dogs and can contribute to poor joint health because of increased stress on the body. Obesity may exacerbate other diseases and conditions, too.

Finding the right food and feeding it in the right amount is not so simple. Though consumers have many choices when it comes to purchasing or making food for their dogs, not all choices are good. If you purchase a food that is not suitable for your Rottweiler, you will know: Your Rottweiler's health may suffer, her coat may become dry and brittle, and her stools may be copious and difficult to pick up. "Rott'n gas," as Rottweiler owners affectionately refer to the horrendous odor that can be released from the dog's gastrointestinal tract, is usually an indicator that the food she is eating is perhaps not being metabolized as well as it should be.

Types of Commercial Food

When selecting a quality commercial food, there are four types of foods that may be available to you: wet or canned, semimoist, dry, and frozen.

Canned: Wet or canned foods usually have the least amount of preservatives in them. Canned foods also have the highest water content, up to 75 percent or more, which may reduce the risk of bloat since canned foods are already wet and do not expand. Canned foods are generally very palatable; dogs love to eat them. On the down side, pound for pound, canned foods are the most expensive way to feed a dog. They also tend to contain a lot of fat. Because the food is soft, they do not offer any teeth-cleaning benefits. Some dogs also have difficulties forming firm stools when eating canned foods.

An alternative to feeding solely canned foods is to mix a portion of canned food with dry kibble.

Semimoist: Though your dog might enjoy the taste of these foods, semimoist foods or those that are promoted as being "chewy" or "meaty" are generally high in sugars. They can also be a bit more expensive than dry kibble, but are less expensive than wet foods. Semimoist foods are typically not recommended by veterinarians because of the high sugar content. Additional problems can include difficulties in forming firm stools, and the fact that this food, similar to the wet foods, does not provide any teeth-cleaning benefits.

Dry: Kibble is a good choice to help prevent tooth decay as the hard bits can help to clean the dog's teeth, much as chewing on a bone would. Dry foods are less expensive and therefore very economical to feed. This food also is low in sugar and contains appropriate amounts of fat. The greatest drawback to dry foods is that they contain the highest amount of preservatives, although most good food manufacturers are moving toward natural preservatives to lessen this problem. Additionally, because the food is dry, it will expand in the dog's stomach. The exact causes for bloat are still not known, but food that expands suddenly in the stomach has been a suspected cause for some time. To counter this problem, some owners will moisten the kibble with water or mix the food with a portion of canned dog food.

Frozen: Commercially made fresh foods are available in some markets. These foods are cooked, frozen, and reasonably priced. They can be thawed, broken into chunks and fed alone, or as a supplement to dry kibble. Storage is the biggest drawback to this food; you'll need an outdoor garage freezer unless you don't mind running to the grocery store on a regular basis.

Quality Guide

Pet foods are required to meet the minimum standards approved by the American Association of Feed Control Officials (AAFCO).

When a food meets the AAFCO minimum standards, it is certified by the AAFCO and can advertise on the package that it is a "complete and balanced" food.

But what is complete and balanced? The key is if the food has undergone feeding trials. If tests have shown that dogs not only maintain good health on the food but actually *thrive* on the food, this is excellent proof that the valuable nutrients in the food are being assimilated and utilized by the dog. Foods that have undergone food trials will show this on the package. Foods that have not undergone feeding trials will be identified as food that has been "formulated" for dogs. This means that *your* dog is the guinea pig that determines the quality of the food. Avoid these foods. The feeding of your Rottweiler should not be an experiment!

Multivitamins and Supplements

A quick look in a pet store or a browse on the Internet reveals a plethora of multivitamin and supplements designed to boost your dog's immune system and promote health. Do they? Or are they even needed?

The verdict is mixed. But there are some definite yeas and nays. One rule is if you are feeding a quality diet to your Rottweiler, you should *never* supplement with calcium—particularly while the Rottweiler is growing. Calcium is thought to exacerbate the symptoms or development of hip dysplasia in predisposed dogs that might have gone symptom free had they not been supplemented with calcium. It can also result in poor conformation, lameness, and skeletal abnormalities.

Another rule is to *always* consult your veterinarian before adding a supplement to your dog's diet, no matter how innocuous the supplement seems. Supplements of specific vitamins, minerals, and other ingredients are frequently used by holistic veterinarians as nutraceuticals. If something has the power to heal, it also has the ability to *harm.*

As for multivitamins, if you choose to add a multivitamin to your dog's diet to "fill in the nutritional cracks," you should do the following:

1. Follow the 20 percent rule. The multivitamin should not contain more than 20 percent of the nutritional minimums set by the AAFCO. The nutrient balance is very delicate and to use a multi-vitamin that contains more than 20 percent could put this balance out of whack, resulting in serious health problems. For example, excess levels of vitamin D can cause diarrhea, dehydration, and even death. Excess zinc, which is a mineral commonly listed in many multivitamins, can block absorption of copper.

2. Look for quality ingredients. Technically, whether a vitamin is from a whole food source or synthetic, the body metabolizes the vitamin in the same way. Some veterinarians and nutritionists feel, however, that vitamins from whole food sources are better than synthetic vitamins in that they are more highly digestible and possibly could be more effective in the body. In other words, a little bit can go a long way, but some vitamins are cost prohibitive in their natural form. The rule here would be to look for natural-sourced vitamins, where possible.

3. Think "chelates." Chelated minerals are preferable to oxides and sulfides that don't metabolize as well. In layman's terms, chelated minerals are nutraceutically based minerals that are wrapped in an amino acid protein. The protein "cover" allows the chelated mineral to pass through the stomach and into the bowels where the mineral can be utilized, rather than being destroyed in the stomach. If the multivitamin contains chelated minerals, it will say so on the label.

4. Be wary of other ingredients. One concern with multivitamins is that some manufacturers seem to be adding everything into the mix to appeal to a wide market. This is not necessarily good. Experts advise reading the label carefully.

5. Consult your veterinarian. First and foremost, before considering adding a multivitamin to your dog's diet, consult your veterinarian. He or she can make recommendations for quality products and/or help you to decipher what is in a product.

Nutritional Needs: Puppies, Adults, Seniors

There is no hard-and-fast rule about how to feed a large-breed puppy, but the current recommendation is to feed a diet that is not too rich in energy (calories). High-calorie diets can cause excessive growth rates and an increased risk of developing skeletal problems. Calcium must also be limited (see Multivitamin and Supplements, pages 107–108), and the calcium/phosphorous ratio (1.2 to 1) must be maintained.

Protein: The protein in the diet of large-breed puppies needs to be a highly digestible, high-quality, meat-based protein, such as chicken, lamb, or egg. Foods using vegetable-based proteins, such as corn, wheat, or soy, are generally cheaper, but these proteins are considered "incomplete." Vegetable-based protein sources don't supply the necessary amino acids required by dogs.

Weight control: Finally, puppies can't be allowed to become pudgy or roly-poly. Excess weight is hard on their developing bodies and can cause development problems.

In order to achieve a steady growth and a healthy weight, breeders and owners may do a variety of things. Commonly, the puppy will receive puppy food only until she is six months old, and then is weaned to adult food. Some breeders will feed puppy food up to six months, wean to adult food for the next several months, and then go back onto puppy food until the puppy is twelve months old. Some manufacturers who are researching the large-breed rapid growth problem are developing and offering puppy foods designed specifically for the large-

or giant-breed puppy. If the foods have passed feeding trials, they could be an excellent choice.

Adult food: When the puppy reaches twelve months, even though she is not fully grown and may not be mature until she is two or three years old, she should be eating adult food. This food can be used as long as the Rottweiler is active.

Food for geriatric dogs: Geriatric dogs are thought to lose some of their ability to digest their food, so many of the valuable nutrients literally pass through the dog's system unused. Foods containing high-quality vitamins and minerals will help to improve absorption. A highly palatable food is also key in the Rottweiler's later years; if she can't taste as well, an inviting food will encourage her to eat, which will ensure she gets the nutrition she needs.

Holistic Diets

The move to natural fresh diets has received a lot of attention in the last few years. Fresh diets consist of meat, vegetables, grains, and supplements. They can be prepared with cooked meat or with raw.

Holistic diets contain few if any preservatives or chemicals, and if prepared correctly, will meet and exceed your Rottweiler's nutritional requirements. Many holistic veterinarians swear by natural diets, saying that if there is one thing you can do that will drastically improve the health of your dog, it is to feed a natural diet.

The difficulty in feeding a natural diet is that the diet must be balanced and prepared correctly. (Many inferior diets are currently being promoted on the Internet and other sources.) Creating a balanced diet from natural ingredients and knowing which supplements to use and in what precise quantities is a science, not an art. Additionally, there are concerns regarding bacteria in raw meats used in raw diets. Whether raw or cooked, fresh diets should be developed under the close supervision of a veterinarian, preferably one who has specialized training in the field of nutrition.

Finding a Nutritionist

If you are serious about working with a fresh diet for your Rottweiler, it would be wise to seek out an expert in the field of nutrition to help you develop a diet that will be most beneficial to your dog. For referrals to veterinarians in your area, consult the following organizations:

American College of Veterinary Nutrition
Department of Large Animal Clinical Sciences
Virginia-Maryland Regional College of Veterinary Medicine
Blacksburg, VA 24061-0442
Phone: (540) 231-3956
Fax: (540) 231-7367

American Academy of Veterinary Nutrition
c/o Dan Carey, DVM, Secretary/Treasurer
6571 State Route 503 North
P.O. Box 189
Lewisburg, OH 45338

Good health begins with good nutrition.

Feeding Guidelines

When to Feed

There are a couple of rules to follow when feeding puppies and adults:

1. You must try to feed your Rottweiler at regular times. Puppies should be fed three times a day up until they are six months old, at which time they can be fed twice a day. The feedings should be spread as equally apart as possible, and you should allow for proper "relief" time afterward. A sample schedule for young puppies might be: feedings at 6:00 A.M., 12 noon, and 6:00 P.M. A sample schedule for an adult could be 6:00 A.M. and 6:00 P.M.

2. You must adjust your Rottweiler's feeding schedule to accommodate any period of heavy exercise. The general philosophy is to give your Rottweiler at least one hour to digest her food *before* she exercises, and not to feed her for at least one hour *after* she exercises. Basically, you want your Rottweiler to have had time to cool down and rehydrate herself before you feed her. There is some concern that feeding too close to periods of exercise may increase the dog's chances of bloating.

How Much to Feed

As mentioned earlier, it is important to keep a puppy trim and not allow her to get overweight. It is equally as important to keep adult dogs in good shape. But, how do you know if you are feeding your Rottweiler too much, just enough, or too little?

To determine where your Rottweiler is in terms of weight, you will need to feel her. Work your way into the coat covering her ribs and push lightly toward her ribs. If you can't feel any ribs, she most likely needs to have her food cut back a bit. You might also want to pick up her exercise if she has become one with the couch.

If you exert pressure and can make out the dog's ribs, she might be just fine. If, of course, you don't have to push to feel the dog's ribs, or if you actually can *see* her ribs, she is not getting enough food.

There are various diseases and conditions that can cause weight gain or weight loss. If your dog appears either too fat or too thin, and the weight change has occurred rather suddenly, you will want to have her health assessed by your veterinarian.

Changing Foods

Sudden changes in diet—switching from one brand of food to another—can cause bouts of diarrhea. In order to switch foods without causing your Rottweiler any distress, use the ten-day plan:

• Work in one part of new food to nine parts of the previous food on the first day.

• On the second day, substitute two parts of new food with eight parts of the previous food.

• Continue working the new food into the previous food until you are feeding entirely new food.

Chapter Eleven

Preventive Care

The importance of quality preventive veterinary care cannot be stressed enough. Regular exercise, good foods, access to fresh water, and diligent grooming and dental hygiene go far in developing and maintaining a healthy, strong dog; however, there are some viruses, bacteria, and parasites that can attack, weaken, or even kill your Rottweiler. Puppies and aging dogs are most susceptible to disease, but even mature dogs in the peak of health can be dealt a lethal blow.

Veterinary Care

With today's veterinary care, there's no reason to allow your Rottweiler to be susceptible to disease and parasites that can easily be prevented and/or treated. Preventive care requires that the owner visit his or her veterinarian at least once a year. Puppies will require a minimum of five visits in their first year, beginning at eight weeks.

Good veterinary care does not come without cost. What you put into preventing diseases and controlling parasites, however, is a small expense compared to treating an illness resulting from lack of preventive care.

Selecting a Veterinarian

If you have previously owned dogs or currently own a dog and have a veterinarian you communicate well with and trust, you're one step ahead of the game. If you don't have a veterinarian, or if you've recently moved and are looking for a new one, there are several ways to find someone you'll enjoy bringing your Rottweiler to for care.

• Call your breeder for suggestions. If he lives in the same town as you do, he will have someone he or she works closely with and trusts.

• Call local breeders. If your breeder lives out of town, she may know of some breeders in your area who could give you a referral to veterinarians they use. You can also tap into the national clubs' referral services to find breeders in your area to call for veterinary referrals.

• Contact the local all-breed club, a training club, and the local humane society or nonprofit shelter. All of these groups have members who

Preventive veterinary care will go far in protecting your Rottweiler from several deadly diseases.

use veterinarians and would certainly share the names of some of their favorites with you.

• Check with neighbors. If you have neighbors, friends, or relatives with healthy dogs, ask them whom they use for a veterinarian.

• Give AAHA a call. The American Animal Hospital Association (AAHA) can give you members' names in your area. To contact AAHA, call: 1-800-252-2242.

Once you have a short list of names, you may want to call a veterinarian who has come with a glowing recommendation and whose office is convenient for you. If after your first appointment you're not really comfortable with that veterinarian, make an appointment to visit

another veterinarian. You shouldn't make hopping from veterinarian to veterinarian a habit, but you need to find one with whom you are comfortable talking and who you feel you could ask any question in the world and he or she wouldn't think you're dumb.

Remember: If you can't talk to your veterinarian openly and freely about any questions you have regarding your Rottweiler's health and behavior, it doesn't matter how experienced the veterinarian is or how many impressive degrees or associations he or she belongs to. You *must* be comfortable with your veterinarian, and your veterinarian should be comfortable with you and working with Rottweilers.

Common Contagious Infections

There are several viruses that are commonly seen in most parts of the United States. These viruses—parvovirus, canine hepatitis, canine distemper, and rabies—all have effective vaccines that can be given to growing puppies and adult dogs to prevent infection and possible death. The vaccinations for these diseases are considered "core" vaccinations because dogs are considered to be at enough risk of coming in contact with them and potentially dying from them to merit a vaccination protocol for the diseases.

An owner who is close to her dog will be more in tune to any physical or behavioral changes that could be early symptoms of disease.

(Rabies vaccination is required by law.)

"Noncore" vaccinations are for diseases that are not considered a danger to most dogs and are administered only at an "at risk" basis. Depending on your area of the country, for example, it may be recommended to vaccinate your Rottweiler for Lyme disease. Noncore vaccinations generally include Lyme disease, leptospirosis and Bordetella/kennel cough.

Core Vaccinations

Parvovirus

Parvovirus is a deadly disease. It frequently attacks young puppies (eight to twelve weeks) with lethal results. In rare cases, older dogs may also be affected.

The most common form of parvovirus is gastrointestinal and causes vomiting, severe bloody diarrhea, lethargy, and loss of appetite. There is no treatment for this disease other than supportive therapies, such as keeping the puppy hydrated and preventing septicemia.

Unfortunately, the Rottweiler experiences much more severe reactions to parvovirus and suffers a higher mortality rate than most other breeds. Additionally, finding an "open window" for the vaccination to produce an immune response is thought to be more difficult with the Rottweiler than with other breeds (see How Vaccines Work, page 115).

How Vaccines Work . . .

Vaccinations are begun when a puppy is between six and eight weeks and continue every three to four weeks up to twenty weeks of age. Puppies in very high-risk situations may require vaccinations more frequently, such as every two weeks through twenty weeks of age.

The reason for the series of vaccinations is not to build up an immunity, but instead to find the first available time at which the puppy's body can make his own antibodies. Young puppies are initially protected by their mother's antibodies, which she passes to her puppies in her milk. Once the puppy is weaned from his mother's milk, he remains immune to the virus for an undetermined amount of time. And this is the problem—the undetermined time.

If the vaccination is given when the puppy is still immune because of the residual effects from his mother, the vaccination will be discarded from the puppy's body without causing the puppy to create his own antibodies.

Rottweiler puppies that are receiving vaccinations can get the disease if they come in contact with the virus after the mother's antibodies have worn off and before the next vaccination is given. Once the vaccination is given, and it is at a time that the puppy no longer carries his mother's antibodies to the disease, the vaccination will do its job and the puppy will become immune. Most breeds of dogs are considered immune after they have received vaccinations at eight and twelve weeks of age. This is not the case for Rottweilers.

For these reasons, it is essential that you protect your Rottweiler by keeping to your veterinarian's recommended inoculation schedule, and preventing your puppy from having contact with dogs that aren't fully vaccinated.

The vaccine for parvovirus is very effective, but depending on the risk of the disease in your area, your veterinarian may recommend that the vaccines be given at closer intervals and/or for a longer time period. Boosters for parvovirus are given when the puppy is a year old, and then every three years thereafter.

Adopted adult Rottweilers with no veterinary vaccination record should also be vaccinated for parvovirus.

Canine Distemper

The canine distemper virus is extremely contagious, often fatal, and generally targets puppies between two months and one year old. As with parvovirus, distemper can be lethal to older, geriatric dogs, as well as healthy adult dogs. Symptoms of canine distemper include fever, sneezing, shaking, and discharges from the nose and mouth. Vomiting and seizures may also

A young Rottweiler may require certain vaccinations, such as that for parvovirus, at closer intervals and for a longer time period, depending on the individual's risk level.

occur. The disease can progress to affect the victim's nervous system.

Distemper lasts up to four weeks, and there is no known cure. Veterinary treatment usually consists of supportive measures to prevent dehydration and the administration of antibiotics to prevent secondary infections. Dogs that have survived canine distemper may have enamel-damaged teeth, and/or develop hard, thickened nose- and footpads. They may also have permanent nervous system damage and vision problems.

Vaccines are available to prevent the disease and are used quite successfully. The vaccines are given to puppies at eight, twelve, and sixteen weeks, and again at one year. After

the first year, booster shots are currently recommended every three years.

Canine Hepatitis

This viral disease affects a dog's liver, kidneys, and eyes. Canine hepatitis can cause vomiting, diarrhea, seizures, and liver and kidney failure.

There is no cure for canine hepatitis. Only supportive treatments can be offered. Vaccines are available to prevent this deadly disease and should be a part of every Rottweiler's vaccination protocol. Puppies typically are given shots at eight, twelve, and sixteen weeks, followed by a final shot at twelve months. After the initial shot sequence is completed, a booster every three years is recommended.

Rabies

Rabies is the most frightening of all canine diseases because it is virtually always fatal if not treated immediately and it can kill humans.

When an animal has rabies, the virus can remain in the body for up to 12 weeks before the animal begins to show signs of illness. Once the virus spreads in the body, it travels through the nerves to the spinal cord and brain, where it multiplies rapidly. The virus invades the salivary glands where it can be passed to another animal through a bite. Transmission of the virus can also be through touching mucous membranes of the eyes, nose, and mouth, and airborne transmission.

Vaccines against rabies for dogs are effective and are required by law. Puppies receive their first rabies shot at 16 weeks, followed by a booster at 12 months. After this, depending on the immunity duration of the vaccine and your state's laws, you will be required to vaccinate your Rottweiler either on an annual basis or every three years.

Additionally, if your Rottweiler is bitten by a wild animal, make sure you report the bite to animal control, and take your dog to the veterinarian immediately to have the wound cleaned. Remember: You can be infected by this virus while handling or cleaning your dog's wounds. Wear gloves and take extreme precautions.

Are Boosters Necessary?

Vaccine manufacturers recommend that booster shots be given on an annual basis for most vaccinations, or in the case of rabies, every one to three years depending on the state.

Are these boosters necessary? Currently, only rabies vaccines are required to perform duration of immunity tests to determine how long after a vaccine is given the animal will be immune to disease. For all other vaccines, the United States Department of Agriculture (USDA) simply requires that *if* a manufacturer does not test a vaccine for duration of immunity, then an annual booster is required.

Experts in veterinary virology feel that many vaccines may last much longer than one year, and perhaps could be effective for the life of the dog. Other vaccines, on the other hand, are thought to require more frequent "boosting" to maintain an immune level.

Noncore Vaccinations

Leptospirosis

This bacterial disease, which can affect dogs, people, and livestock, can cause fatal damage to the kidneys and liver. The disease can be treated with antibiotics. Leptospirosis can be prevented by keeping dogs out of contact with contaminated water sources and potential carriers of the disease, such as mice, rats, skunks, opossums, raccoons, and voles, and domestic animals, such as pigs, horses, and cows, or by vaccinating dogs that are considered most at risk for contracting the disease.

Currently, vaccines protect against only four of the eight serovars or strains that appear to be most troublesome for dogs. In the past, there have been concerns with the number of adverse reactions to the leptospirosis vaccines, but recent advances in 2000 have produced a different sort of vaccine that is thought to produce far fewer adverse responses. As with all vaccines, consult with your veterinarian about what the risks for the actual disease are for your Rottweiler and balance these with the risks of the vaccine.

Lyme Disease

Lyme disease begins with a bite from an infected deer or black-legged tick that may be no bigger than a pinhead. The disease is caused by a spiral-shaped bacterium bent on destruction. Signs of Lyme disease in dogs are usually marked by a fever, loss of appetite, and lameness where there has been no previous disease or injury. Relapses can develop weeks and months after the initial bout with the disease.

The longer the disease goes untreated, the more difficult it is to get it under control. Antibiotics are used to treat Lyme disease and are very effective if the treatment is begun in the early stages of the disease.

Prevention of the disease may include a vaccination schedule for Lyme disease, but should also include commonsense precautions. If you live in areas where the disease is prevalent—mid-Atlantic, Northeast, North Central, and Pacific coastal regions—you might consider having your dog tested for Lyme disease in the spring and fall. Topical tick repellents for dogs may also help to prevent exposure to an infected tick, and therefore to this disease.

If you find a deer tick on your dog, capture the tick, without being bitten yourself, and bag it in a ziplock bag. Take the live tick to your veterinarian to be tested for Lyme disease. And, of course, if your dog develops symptoms, have him examined. The deer ticks are so tiny that often they can bite your dog without your even knowing it.

Parainfluenza/Bordetella (Kennel Cough)

Kennel cough is a generic term that encompasses several diseases causing respiratory problems, primarily Parainfluenza, *Bordetella bronchiseptica*, and mycoplasma. Interestingly, one or more of these diseases is usually involved in kennel cough and there is rarely just one organism at work.

The disease typically lasts between 14 to 20 days in which the infected dog coughs—a lot. The dog may cough to the point of vomiting. He may also have a watery, nasal discharge. In severe cases, he may develop a fever, become lethargic, develop pneumonia, and even die. Most deaths occur with immuno-compromised adults or young puppies that have not been vaccinated.

If the infection is mild, kennel cough is not treated. If the infection is more severe and coughing is frequent and harsh, medications may be prescribed to help control the dog's coughing and make him more comfortable. In serious cases, antibiotics and bronchodilators may be prescribed.

Kennel cough vaccine is generally given to puppies at eight or twelve weeks, and then at twelve months. Dogs that are boarded regularly, attend training classes, or travel to shows may require receiving the vaccine every six months.

Internal Parasites

Worms

Often, a healthy adult Rottweiler may be able to safely coexist with a mild infestation of worms; however, most dogs and especially puppies are not in optimal health when worms of any kind are present. The following are five types of worms that can wreak havoc with your Rottweiler's health.

Hookworm: This bloodsucker attaches to the dog's small intestine. Hookworms can cause bloody stools, diarrhea, anemia, and even death. Puppies can be infected by drinking their infected mother's milk.

Older puppies and dogs can become infected by ingesting eggs found in feces, or by the worm's larvae penetrating the dog's skin. Using a heartworm preventive that includes medication for this worm will prevent an infestation. Dogs with worms present can be given a wormer.

Roundworm: The eggs from this worm are passed through the feces and must be ingested. Heavy infestations *can* kill puppies and dogs. Symptoms are a bloated-looking belly, a dull coat, vomiting, and diarrhea. Roundworms can be controlled by using a heartworm preventive that includes medication for roundworms as well. Dogs and puppies infested with roundworms can be wormed, though it may take a series of wormings to get rid of all worms.

Parasites, both internal and external, are present everywhere—just waiting for a host...

Tapeworm: Fleas are the most common carrier of tapeworms in dogs. Additionally, if your Rottweiler likes to chase rabbits and rodents, he might come in contact with an animal that is carrying this worm. Tapeworms can cause vomiting and diarrhea. Parts of the worm will be shed in the dog's stool, and little ricelike larvae can be found crawling around the dog's anal region. A wormer for tapeworm is effective in ridding the dog of this parasite. Consult your veterinarian.

Whipworm: Whipworm can be difficult to diagnose because the eggs of the worm are not shed continuously in the dog's stool. Once the eggs are found, it can be difficult to rid the dog of these parasites. The eggs of the whipworm can live years after they have been shed, so dogs often reinfect themselves. A series of wormings is necessary to rid a dog of the infestation. A monthly preventive that is combined with heartworm preventive is available from your veterinarian.

Heartworm: An infestation with this worm can kill many dogs. Heartworm is transmitted by mosquitos infected with heartworm larvae. Once the larvae enter the bloodstream, they travel to the heart where they lodge themselves and mature into adult worms. Symptoms of heartworm include a persistent cough, losing consciousness, loss of weight, coughing blood, and weakness. Many dogs have undergone treatment for heartworm and survived, but the success of the treatment depends on the age and health of the dog, and the extent of the infestation.

A much easier approach is to prevent this lethal parasite from ever gaining a foothold. Puppies can begin heartworm preventive as early as eight weeks—and should do so! Adult dogs are tested for heartworms annually and then given a monthly or daily preventive.

Giardia

In addition to worms, there is another internal parasite that Rottweiler owners need to be aware of—*giardia*. As more Rottweilers and their owners discover the fun and excitement of backpacking, camping, and hiking, more dogs will be exposed to *giardia*. Even those owners who don't take their dogs into the country may find that their dogs have been exposed.

Giardia is a microscopic parasite found in streams and rivers. An infected dog may become bloated in the abdominal region, vomit, and have severe and bloody diarrhea. The parasite can attack with no mercy and has been known to kill untreated dogs and puppies very quickly. Quick veterinary treatment is effective in eradicating this parasite.

Zoonotic Diseases

Some worms are zoonotic and can affect the health of family members. Roundworms, tapeworms, and hookworms can all infect humans—some with serious health consequences. The parasite *giardia* is also zoonotic and can cause disease in humans.

Fortunately, most zoonotic diseases can be prevented in humans with good hygiene. (Wash those hands!)

External Parasites

Fleas, ticks, and mites make up the most commonly seen external parasites. Depending on the area of the country you live in, these parasites may be a seasonal problem or a year-round one. Control of these parasites is important because all three can compromise your dog's health. Additionally, fleas and ticks can be carriers of several illnesses, including Lyme disease (ticks) and Black Plague (fleas), and parasites, such as tapeworms (fleas).

Fortunately, there are effective ways to prevent or eradicate infestations of these pests.

Fleas

Fleas are carriers of disease and tapeworm infection. With the Rottweiler's thick black coat, you are more likely to see the effects the fleas have on your dog first—itching and scratching—before finding a flea.

If your dog has an allergy to fleas—and this is not uncommon—the scratching will be much more severe and your dog may become very uncomfortable. One flea bite may be all your dog needs to develop a significant allergic reaction.

The cycle: Fleas also have a nasty tendency to take a ride in on

A healthy Rottweiler is a happy Rottweiler and makes a great jogging buddy.

your dog and set up camp in your home. Once the fleas have a steady source of blood (your Rottweiler's) they mature rapidly and lay eggs on your dog, your dog's bedding, the carpets, and rugs, and even in furniture. When these eggs hatch, there's a whole new batch of fleas to contend with. Unless you eradicate the fleas as they hatch, but before they begin laying eggs, you won't be able to stop the cycle. There are many products on the market to help kill off adult fleas before they are able to reproduce. Consult your veterinarian about the efficacy and safety of products that can be used on your Rottweiler, but note that young puppies will not be able to use all products. You can also use a flea comb to help catch adult fleas.

Your home: For your home, a *thorough* vacuuming on a daily basis can be a very efficient and safe way to rid your home of fleas. After vacuuming, don't forget to remove the bag and tie it tightly in a plastic bag that will not allow the fleas to escape. There are also products that can be used to treat your carpets, but be sure to use extreme caution. Any chemical or substance that is toxic to fleas is likely to be toxic to humans and dogs.

Prevention: Flea preventives are all over the market. Some are sold as over-the-counter products and require no prescription from the veterinarian; others can be obtained only with a veterinarian's prescription. The flea preventives available from your veterinarian that come as a liquid and are applied topically to the dog's skin are very effective in preventing fleas from even taking a bite. These products can be very helpful, particularly to dogs with an allergy to fleas. Flea preventives also come in oral forms.

Not all flea preventives can be used on young puppies. Consult with your veterinarian for safe ways of preventing fleas from using your puppy as a host. If you have an adult, it would be wise to ask your veterinarian for a flea preventive recommendation as well. With new products entering the market and studies following the efficacy and side effects of current products, your veterinarian will be able to guide you toward the safest products.

Ticks

Ticks suck blood, and they can cause allergic reactions or even paralysis to the saliva in their bites. Tick bites can be deep and can result in secondary bacterial infections. They are also hosts to a variety of diseases, such as Lyme disease, Rocky Mountain spotted fever, Babesiosis, and Ehrlichiosis.

As with fleas, ticks can be difficult to spot on your Rottweiler's coat. If you brush your dog regularly, you are likely to spot a large tick. Ticks often like to attach to a dog's ears, which are a bit easier to see. If you've been out for a walk or live in an area that has ticks, be sure to check your Rottweiler from head to toe daily during the peak tick season—spring.

Depending on the area of the country you live in, fleas may be a year-round concern.

Removal: If you find a tick, use tweezers to grab the tick as closely as possible to the tick's head. Pull straight out, without any twisting, to attempt to pull the tick's head out as well. Wash the wound with soap and water and apply an antiseptic. Even if your Rottweiler has had tick bites before, watch for swelling around the throat area or hives, which would signal that he is having an allergic reaction to the bite. If an allergic reaction occurs, rush your dog to the veterinarian. The swelling may become so severe as to cut off your dog's breathing.

If the tick you have removed appears to be a deer tick, place the tick in a reclosable plastic bag and take it to your veterinarian for testing. These ticks are notorious for carrying Lyme disease. If other tick-borne diseases are prevalent in your area, discuss the symptoms of these diseases with your veterinarian and follow up with testing if he or she advises it.

Prevention: Topical tick preventives are available that are very effective in preventing ticks from biting your dog. Collars with tick preventive on them are also available. Talk to your veterinarian about using these products during peak tick season, and the use of these products in other seasons if you engage in many activities with your dog in the wilderness or country. Keep in mind, too, that young puppies may not be able to use tick preventive products safely until they are older and bigger. Follow the advice of your veterinarian.

Mites

There are various types of mites, but the ones that are most frequently seen is demodex mites. These mites live in the Rottweiler's hair follicles and sebaceous glands. They are seen as patches of red, hairless areas. An infestation of demodex mites is often referred to as "red mange."

Mange can usually be controlled by medications, an improved diet, and a reduction in the dog's stress. (Stress is believed to be a factor in why some puppies or dogs fall prey to this type of mange and others don't.) Mange may also be a sign of a compromised immune system.

Regardless, red mange is not something you want to have affect your Rottweiler. If you suspect your dog might have this form of mange, seek veterinary assistance as soon as possible.

Chapter Twelve

Common Diseases of the Rottweiler

The Rottweiler, prior to its soaring rise in popularity in the 1980s, was a very healthy breed with relatively few problems. As with any breed that reaches the pinnacle of popularity—the Rottweiler was ranked number two in AKC registrations for years—when the numbers of dogs bred increases, the number of health problems often increases as well. This is due in large part to breeders who are not careful in screening their dogs for hereditary diseases.

Breeding and Testing

Of course, not all the blame can be put on irresponsible breeders. Some diseases and conditions have no known genetic basis. Other diseases appear to have some genetic basis but may be greatly influenced by diet, exercise, and environment. Across the United States there are scores of breeders who carefully track and screen for virtually every known potential problem and are still heartbroken when a dog dies of

cancer or a promising show dog is diagnosed with hip dysplasia.

Careful breeding and testing go far in tracking and breeding out certain diseases, but there are no absolute guarantees. For this reason, even if you have purchased your Rottweiler from the very best of breeders, it is wise to know what types of diseases are associated with the Rottweiler, what the symptoms are, and what treatments are available. Hopefully, your Rottweiler will never be ill, but if she is, you may be a little better equipped at recognizing the problem and seeking veterinary help quickly.

Deadly Problems

Of the greatest concern to Rottweiler owners are diseases that are lethal to their dogs. The most common of these diseases is, unfortunately, cancer.

Cancer—The Number One Killer

Rottweilers can fall prey to a variety of cancers, some of which can be treated surgically or in combination with chemotherapy and radiation. Veterinarians involved in cancer treatment relate that the key to survival or a significantly prolonged, quality life is early detection.

Osteosarcomas: One type of cancer, osteosarcomas, or bone cancers, currently do not have a very good survival rate. This is one of the most aggressive of cancers, and it is occurring in Rottweilers with increasing frequency. Osteosarcoma previously has been recorded as attacking older dogs and Rottweilers as young as five years old, but more recent information indicates that the age at which Rottweilers are now suffering from this disease can be as young as two or three years old.

The Rottweiler Health Foundation (RHF) is funding research into osteosarcomas, including efforts into researching cancer suppresser genes.

Symptoms of osteosarcoma include mild lameness and swelling near the shoulder or stifle joint, two common areas in which the tumor may begin developing. Untreated, a cancerous Rottweiler may die within six months or require euthanasia to relieve her of the overwhelming pain, since the cancer quickly spreads to other parts of the body.

Treatment for the cancer can include amputation of the limb; however, some veterinary oncologists are developing alternative methods to prolong the dog's life and provide a longer period of pain-free and quality living. Treatment is expensive. There are no guarantees, and the outcome is invariably the same.

Rottweiler Health Foundation

The Rottweiler Health Foundation (RHF) has been instrumental in supporting several studies through the Canine Health Foundation in cancer and hip dysplasia. To learn more about how you can help support this crucial health research and help improve the health of the breed in the future, contact the RHF at 281-955-2747, or visit the RHF's web site: *www.RottweilerHealth.org.* Your donation or assistance could make a difference in the future of tomorrow's Rottweiler.

Hopefully, the future will provide an effective way of wiping out this disease, or preventive measures either through genetics or environment, or both, to avoid this lethal disease.

Other cancers: Regularly check your dog for lumps or bumps under the skin, and if you find any, have your veterinarian look at them. Some cancers can be surgically removed and/or treated with chemotherapy and radiation. Your dog's only chance, however, is if the cancer is detected early.

Beyond bumps, if you detect any changes in your dog's appetite, mood, or behavior, such as panting, lethargy, or restlessness, seek the advice of a veterinarian. The early warning signs of cancer are subtle.

Subaortic Stenosis

This heart problem is a congenital defect, meaning it is found at birth.

Puppies from healthy parents that are tested and registered free of genetic diseases have a greater chance of being healthy themselves.

Subaortic stenosis (SAS) is considered to be hereditary. For this reason, it is important when purchasing a Rottweiler to make sure both parents are clear of the disease. Since testing for SAS is fairly new, the Rottweiler's grandparents may not have been tested, but if they are, and they're clear of the disease, this is a tremendous plus.

SAS involves the presence of scarlike tissue underneath the aortic valve in the aorta as it leaves the heart's left ventricle. This narrowing of the aorta makes it extremely difficult for blood to be pushed out of the heart and through the aorta. The pressure at which the heart has to pump the blood through this narrow aorta causes the heart's muscle to thicken or increase in size to compensate. The enlarged heart can in turn cause problems with the heart's rhythm.

Symptoms: Dogs with mild cases of SAS or little scarring of the aorta may show no symptoms and live a full life. Dogs with a more extensively narrowed aorta may develop only moderate symptoms and may also live a full life but may have some exercise limitations. On the other hand, puppies born with severe narrowing of the aorta can suddenly die at six to eight months. Others may survive until they are adults, and then die with no warning.

Treatment: A Rottweiler diagnosed with SAS has few treatment options. Dogs with moderate and serious SAS may be able to benefit from medications. Surgery to correct the problem is being performed at a handful of veterinary colleges, but the surgery is expensive and may not be a reasonable alternative for many owners. As more is learned about the disease, perhaps veterinary medicine will provide Rottweiler breeders and owners with better ways to prevent and treat the disease.

The Orthopedic Foundation for Animals (OFA) has a cardiac registry in which it categorizes the condition of the dog's heart, as well as who examined the dog. An examination by a board-certified veterinary cardiologist is generally considered more accurate than that by a general practitioner.

Bloat

Canine Gastric Dilation-Volvulus (GDV) or *bloat* is deadly. The exact

The two greatest killers of Rottweilers are cancer followed by subaortic stenosis.

causes of bloat are mostly a mystery. The disease itself involves the dog's stomach becoming distended with air and beginning to twist. The twisting action of the stomach acts as a clamp that shuts down the flow of gases, fluids, food, and blood into the intestines. Once the stomach is twisted too tightly, the blood supply is choked off and the dog can be dead within a few hours.

Susceptibility: Breeds that are particularly susceptible seem to be large dogs—more than 45 pounds (20 kg). This is a condition that can and *does* affect Rottweilers, though, and with lethal results, so Rottweiler owners need to be aware of the disease.

Currently, there seem to be at least four factors in determining which dogs might be more susceptible to bloat than others: age, temperament, the depth/width ratio of the dog's chest within the breed, and a history of bloat in the family.

The depth/width ratio of the dog's chest within the breed, not compared to other breeds, may also play a role in which dogs are predisposed to this condition and which are not. A history of bloat in the family is thought to be another factor in the bloat equation. Dogs with littermates or parents that have suffered from bloat have an increased chance of bloating themselves.

And finally, temperament is believed to affect which dogs suffer from bloat and which dogs do not. Anxious, fearful or depressed people have been shown to swallow air and then burp it back up—a condition called *aerophagia*. Aerophagia has been observed in several large and giant-breed dogs suffering from recurring gastric dilation. A direct relationship between aerophagia and bloat has not yet been made; however, the general feeling is that the more chance there is for air to enter the stomach, the more likely the dog might be to bloat.

Symptoms: Dogs suffering from bloat require immediate veterinary attention. As many as 30 percent of bloat sufferers die, so there is no time to waste seeking help. Symptoms of bloat include
• abdominal swelling
• circling or restlessness
• panting, drooling
• the affected dog looking anxiously at its sides

Prevention: Until the exact causes or factors involved in bloat are found, preventing this disease

If you plan on participating in performance sports or will be physically active with your Rottweiler in any way, it is important to be aware of the signs of heat stroke.

will be difficult; however, in the meantime
• It is advisable to feed your Rottweiler two or three smaller meals a day rather than one large meal.
• Rubber toys can be placed in the food bowl to force your Rottweiler to slow her eating; if she's not gulping food, perhaps less air will enter her stomach.
• Constant access to fresh, cool water should be provided to avoid gulping great quantities or gorging on water after a meal.
• Moistening kibble or a mixing dry and wet (canned) food together might help to decrease the amount of swelling in the dog's stomach.
• Owners should also keep abreast of the latest developments with bloat. As research is completed, the above preventives may be modified. Consult with your veterinarian for the most up to date information.

Heatstroke

Because of their large size and black coats, Rottweilers may be a little more prone to heatstroke than dogs of lighter builds and fairer-colored coats—tan, blonde, or white. If you plan on being active with your dog, and you live in an area that can get quite warm in the summer, you should know the basics of preventing heatstroke and treatment.

Signs of heatstroke include
• rapid panting
• sudden weakness or tiredness
• high temperature (above 105°F, or 40.6°C)
• dark red to purple gums and tongue

PRA can be diagnosed by an ophthalmoscopic examination and a process called electroretinography. There is no cure for PRA. Affected dogs should not be bred.

Puppy buyers searching for a PRA-free Rottweiler, should look for parents that have been examined recently (within 12 months) by a board-certified veterinary ophthalmologist and registered as free of eye disease with the Canine Eye Registry Foundation (CERF) (write ARC, page 159, for address). Having parents that are free of PRA does not, of course, guarantee a PRA-free Rottweiler. PRA is considered a recessive trait, so a Rottweiler may have the genetic capacity to give offspring PRA (the dog is a carrier of PRA), but does not have PRA herself.

von Willebrand's Disease

This disease is hereditary and affects the dog's ability to properly form blood clots.

Symptoms of vWD can include bruising, nosebleeds, or toenails that when quicked just won't stop bleeding. Bleeding can occur in the stomach or intestine, which will result in black or tarry (blood-containing) stools. A dog may have blood in her urine. Bleeding in the joints will cause lameness.

Dogs can be tested for this disease. Those with the disease should not be bred, and, if you're searching for a puppy with the best chance of *not* having any health problems, you'll want to make sure your puppy comes from stock that is free of this disease, too.

Treatment: Treatment for this disease includes blood transfusions from dogs with normal clotting abilities. Some dogs with vWD may also have hypothyroidism (see page 131) and will benefit from treatment of this disease. Recent studies indicate that there may be drugs available to help dogs overcome bleeding episodes. One such drug is applied intranasally but whether this drug is effective is still inconclusive. If your Rottweiler suffers from this disease, be sure to keep track of the latest strides made in helping vWD dogs.

Other Diseases and Injuries

The following diseases, conditions, and injuries can occur in Rottweilers, and owners should be aware of what the symptoms are in case they should ever arise.

Allergies

Dogs in general, Rottweilers included, can suffer from a variety of allergies. Grass, pollen, food, plastic, insect bites, and fleas are major sources of allergies among canines. Symptoms can range from constant scratching, excessive licking, hot spots, and ear infections, to swelling, angioedema (swelling of the face), or even death from swollen and obstructed airways (anaphylaxis).

Allergies can be determined through food, skin, and blood testing.

Treatment of an allergy may be as simple as changing foods, such as switching to a lamb-based diet if the Rottweiler is allergic to chicken, or may involve a more complex regime of medications, including antihistamines, fatty acid supplements, biotin, and corticosteroids.

Cruciate Ligament Rupture

The most common knee injury for the Rottweiler is a ruptured cruciate ligament. The injury is most likely to occur when the knee joint twists, as when a Rottweiler loses her balance on a slick floor or ice, or makes a hard turn while running. This sudden and forceful twisting motion puts too much pressure on the ligament that stretches across the front of the knee, causing it to tear.

Once the ligament is torn, the dog will be in pain and will hold up her leg. If the tear is determined to be complete, the ligament must be reattached through surgery. The most difficult part of the Rottweiler's recovery is keeping her quiet for the six to eight weeks that the ligament requires to heal properly. If the tear is partial or if the Rottweiler is older and may not survive the surgery, antiinflammatories and a gentle exercise regime such as swimming may be prescribed.

Ear Infections

Rottweilers are not more prone to ear infections than other dogs; however, because Rottweilers and their owners tend to be quite active and may take part in a variety of sports that might expose the dogs to more water, woods, and country than other breeds, it is important for owners to recognize the causes and early signs of ear infections.

Ear infections that are in both ears are often the result of an allergy. Ear infections that occur in only ear are most often the result of a foreign body such as a burr, thorn, or tick that has entered the dog's ear canal and upset the natural delicate balance of yeast and bacteria. Dogs' ears also do not drain well, so any contact with water in which the dog cannot shake the water out may result in an ear infection.

Symptoms: Symptoms of ear infections include shaking head or ears, as if to get something out, scratching ears, a foul smell from the ears, and unusual amounts of discharge from the ear. In severe cases, the dog may lose her balance or be disoriented. All ear infections require prompt veterinary care. If allowed to progress untreated, the ear infection can work its way from the outer ear, into the middle and even inner ear with serious and sometimes irreversible results.

Epilepsy

Epilepsy is a generic term that covers virtually all forms of seizures. If there is no known underlying cause for the seizures, either by injury or a disease, the seizures are considered "idiopathic" or primary epilepsy. Idiopathic epilepsy generally occurs in dogs between six months and five years, though the starting age is generally around two

Good preventive care can be a major factor in protecting your Rottweiler from succumbing to the many diseases and parasites that once took their toll of the canine population.

to three years. Dogs with this form of epilepsy should never be bred. Idiopathic epilepsy is believed to be inherited and has been shown to be familial.

Dogs that begin having seizures after the age of five are generally considered to have something causing the epilepsy. In order to stop the seizures in these cases, the source of the epilepsy—the disease that is causing the condition—must be cured or controlled. Seizures in this instance can result from head injuries, an infection, or exposure to toxins, such as antifreeze or lead. Seizures may also occur if the dog is suffering from kidney or liver failure,

or if the dog has low oxygen levels in the blood, for example from heart disease, such as SAS (see pages 125–126). Tumors can also be a cause of seizures.

Treatment: If no disease is present, or the disease cannot be cured or controlled, the goal of veterinary treatment becomes to control the seizures. Many medications are available to help control seizures; however, treatment is typically restricted to more severe cases—those that have frequent seizures or seizures that are long in duration—because the medications themselves can have serious side effects at higher doses and over a longer time period.

Chapter Thirteen

The Basics of a Well-behaved Rottweiler

As a large breed that can tip the scales at 100 pounds (45 kg) or more, the Rottweiler *must* be taught at an early age the basics of socially acceptable behavior. Puppies must learn to pay attention when their names are spoken and to sit on command within the first few weeks. As the puppy matures, he must be taught additional skills, such as walking nicely on a leash, which is necessary for control when the dog becomes full grown.

Why Train Your Rottweiler?

In addition to simply being able to manage a dog of this size, the Rottweiler owner must be able to deal with and counter the unfair reputation that the Rottweiler has as a mean, evil dog. This notion is, of course, simply not true. But, the responsibility to make sure that your Rottweiler is impeccably trained and well socialized with children and adults of all races is critically important.

As a Rottweiler owner, you are responsible and liable for your dog's actions. Today's society requires that the Rottweiler must have more sense than his owner when dealing with some potentially complex situations. In order to give your dog the skills he will need to have to be a good canine citizen, you must have the skills to train your Rottweiler.

Fortunately, the Rottweiler is not a difficult dog to train and typically *lives* for his training sessions with his owner. However, when training your Rottweiler, it is important to always know what kind of dog you are working with, and to respect him for his differences.

Six Rottweiler Training Rules

The Rottweiler is not like other dogs in many ways. When training a Rottweiler, many of these differences surface. Your understanding of the breed's unique qualities and how you handle them will make a difference in how quickly your Rottweiler learns.

1. Forget "Alpha," Think Leader

The biggest mistake you can make with your Rottweiler is to attempt to train him using the bully method. Forget all that you've read about abusing your dog physically in the name of "alpha," because that's what it is—abuse. Attempting to throw your dog to the ground in an "alpha" roll, grabbing him by the scruff on his neck, smacking him under the chin, or whipping him with the leash are all forms of abuse. Your Rottweiler is smart enough to know this. As German breeder Franz Menacher of Landsberg, Germany says, "Training a Rottweiler is like raising a child. If you beat your child, he can take only so much." Menacher emphasizes that the way to train a Rottweiler is with positive reinforcement. (More on this later.)

It is true that the Rottweiler is a dominant dog by nature. He will take over a household if no one is there to show him that he is most useful as second in command. How do you establish being a leader? Through training. It is generally this easy. Working with your Rottweiler once a day for even just ten minutes *for the life of the dog* will reinforce on a daily basis that *you* are in command. Generally, owners who practice this regime will never have a problem with their Rottweilers.

2. This Is an Intelligent Dog

The Rottweiler is extremely intelligent and therefore learns commands very quickly. But this exceptional intelligence means an owner must work at keeping training interesting and fun for the dog. When owners have problems with their dogs "unlearning" commands, it is usually because the dog has become bored, the owners have not been consistent in either how they give the command or how they ask the dog to respond to the command.

Finding a good trainer and training school are important to both you and your dog.

3. Rottweilers Remember All

Remembering everything he is taught can certainly be a good trait for training. However, it can also have its drawbacks, because you must be sure your are teaching precisely the response or behavior you want the *first* time. It's not such a great trait if you have members of the family who allow certain behaviors that you don't. For example, if one person allows the Rottweiler to jump on the couch, the Rottweiler will remember; he will never forget that that individual allows him on the couch and he might also think that you should, too. This is generally where the problems

Training Tools for Adults

If you have adopted an adult dog that has had no leash training, you could be in for a challenge. Before you allow a trainer to talk you into pulling out the heavy artillery, such as a prong collar, find a trainer who is adept at using a head halter. This training device looks similar to a horse's halter and follows the same theory—where the head goes, so will the body. The head halter, if used correctly and fitted properly, is a painless but effective training device. Its key benefit is that it gives even the smallest owner gentle control over her dog. And, the device gets the dog's attention. When an owner has his or her dog's attention, *this* is when the training can begin.

can start. Also, if you think you can allow your Rottweiler to do something "just once," think again. A Rottweiler remembers!

4. Transgressions Don't Go Unnoticed

If we could peer into the Rottweiler's brain, we'd probably find he's probably taking detailed notes on the character qualities of every person he meets. A Rottweiler—even as a puppy—will remember people who have not treated him well, so it is critical that his meetings with people stay always positive.

5. Consistency and Positive Reinforcement

Positive reinforcement training, which rewards desired behavior with praise, treats, or toys, is the ideal method to use when working with a Rottweiler because it never directly confronts the Rottweiler's natural instinct to be dominant, but rather shapes appropriate behaviors as the owner earns respect as the dog's leader. Harsh training methods, on the other hand, do *not* work with Rottweilers and should be avoided.

6. Socialization Is Key

Some owners mistakenly think that if they socialize their Rottweilers with lots of different people and dogs, their Rottweilers will be reduced to emotional mush and will never protect them when a dire situation arises. This is foolish and insults the intelligence of the Rottweiler.

Owning a friendly, even outgoing Rottweiler will not diminish your

Rottweiler's natural guarding instincts. If you have any questions about this, talk to anyone who has owned Rottweilers for many years. These dogs will not let you down and will literally die for you, if that's what it takes to keep you safe. There's never been a dog with a larger heart or more devotion than the Rottweiler. But *do* raise him to be the well-socialized dog he was meant to be.

Finding a Good Training School

Though this book will give you the basics you will need to begin training a young puppy that is not old enough to attend training classes, a good training school is a must. Under the skilled supervision of an experienced trainer, you will receive training yourself, and your dog will benefit from socialization with other dogs and working under different surroundings.
• To find a good training school, ask your veterinarian, breeders, the local humane society, and friends with well-trained dogs what school they recommend.
• Call the school to inquire about classes and ask if you can attend a session.
• It is important that you feel comfortable with the trainer and his or her training methods, which should be all positive reinforcement. If you see choke chains being used on puppies or manhandling of adult dogs, don't walk, *run* out of the class. Look for gentle training techniques using food as lures, and praise, treats, and toys as rewards.

• Look for participants (dogs and humans) who are having a great time, because this is what training is all about . . . fun!

Basic Training

Though your Rottweiler will be eager to learn as many commands as you want to teach him, the following are the basic building blocks to more advanced commands.

Name

Both puppies and newly adopted rescue dogs should be taught to respond to their names. Animal behaviorists have shown through

No Name?

In some fast-paced sports, such as agility, there is no time for a name before a command—there's barely time to get the command out. This is not a problem, of course, for the well-trained dog. Once a dog reaches a certain level of training, he will be very focused on you; this attentiveness is one of the great attributes of this breed. When you are at the point where your dog is paying a high level of attention to you, you will find that you won't need to use your dog's name before every command. Before you get to this point, however, it is important to make sure that you have your Rottweiler's attention by saying his name.

studies that setting a dog up with a name and then a command is much more effective than the command without a name first.

• To teach your Rottweiler his name, wait until he is fairly quiet and say his name, *"Schnitzel!"* in a positive and fun way. The tone should make the dog anticipate that something fun is about to happen. When he looks at you, reward him with praise and a treat.

• Continue working on teaching your Rottweiler his name until when you say, *"Schnitzel!"* he immediately locks into your eyes expectantly. When he reaches this point, you can begin to phase out the treats and reward him with verbal and physical praise.

Release

Most people give their dogs this command naturally, but it doesn't

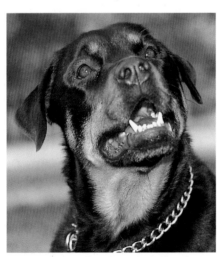

Be sure to use the release command so your Rottweiler knows the exercise is finished.

hurt to remind owners that if you give a dog a command, you must also "release" him from the command. Most dogs recognize *"O.K.!"* or *"Yes!"* as a release command very quickly if the owner also indicates the exercise is over with his or her body language. Raising your hands and giving the release command in an excited, happy voice is usually all it takes for a Rottweiler to share in your enjoyment. Follow this up with lots of physical and verbal praise and a little treat, and your Rottweiler will have this training command down pat.

Sit

The *sit* is a very convenient command. It can be used to settle an excited dog, or to keep a dog from jumping up on someone. In keeping with the leadership role, Rottweiler owners should always require their dogs to sit before receiving a treat, when waiting to be fed, before going out the door, and so on. In other words, this simple command can be used to make your Rottweiler work and thereby continue to cement the leadership/companion roles.

• To teach the *sit,* have your dog stand at your left side. Gently hold his collar with your left hand. Take your right hand and close your fingers around a small treat.

• Say your dog's name, *"Schnitzel!"*

• When you have his attention, say *"Sit!"* As you give the command, hold the treat directly in front of his nose and slowly pass it over his muzzle, past his eyes, and toward

the crown of his head. Your hand should just barely pass above the dog's head. As you move the treat over your Rottweiler's head he will rock back and tuck his hind end under into a *sit*.

• When he is sitting, give him the treat and reward him with lots of love and praise. He is a very good boy!

• Continue practicing this command as often as you can. It won't be long before he will recognize the command and automatically sit. At this point you will no longer need to use the treat as a lure, but you should continue to use the treat as a reward.

Eventually, you can phase out the treat rewards so that your Rottweiler gets rewarded during each session of practicing the *sit* command, but not

The Rottweiler will naturally follow the treat and rock back to "sit."

Slowly bring the treat down and slightly forward to lure your Rottweiler into a "down."

as frequently; perhaps a reward after every three of four *sits* will suffice.

Down

The *down* command is an excellent command for keeping your Rottweiler quiet during your dinner or when you are answering the door. It can also be helpful on walks if your dog tends to be a little dog aggressive; barking or growling in the *down* is much more difficult for the dog than when standing. The *down* is also used in a number of performance events.

• To teach the *down,* use a food lure for positioning.

• With your dog in a *sit,* say his name, *"Schnitzel!"* and then say *"Down!"* as you take a food lure that is wrapped in your right hand and move it from his nose slowly down and out a little bit toward the floor.

• As he follows the treat, he will naturally lie down. If he tries to stand to get the treat, put him back in a *sit,* and begin the exercise again.

Hint: The way in which you lower the treat to the floor can affect how well the dog goes down. If the treat is too close to the dog, he will stand up to back up.

As with the *sit,* use food lures for positioning until your Rottweiler automatically lies down when you say, *"Schnitzel* (pause for attention), *down!"* Continue to reward the correct response to the *down* command with treats and praise. When your Rottweiler is solid on his *downs* with the treat, begin phasing out the treat until you are treating the dog only every four or five times.

Stay

The *stay* command can be taught for either the *sit* or the *down* or both. The technique is the same. Some find that the *down-stay* is easiest to teach initially. The *stay* command is very useful in keeping control of your dog. Note, however, that you should *never* test your dog on the *stay* command in an open or unfenced area. Work initially on lead. You may progress to off-leash work in a controlled area, such as a room in a home. As your Rottweiler becomes steady in his *stay,* you can work outdoors with a long line. Some performance events test the dog's ability to work off leash with the *stay* command as one of the required elements. This is, of course, at a higher level than what you'll be working on initially with your puppy or rescued Rottweiler. So don't rush things—if your Rottweiler figures out he can break his *stay* and run off and play, then you have taken two steps backward. Set your Rottweiler up for success.

• To teach the initial stages of the *stay* command, put your dog on leash in a *sit.* You can also use a *down* command, but for simplicity only the *sit* will be used in this instruction.

• Hold the leash lightly in your right hand and keep your left hand relaxed and by your side.

• Using your left hand, give your dog the *stay* hand signal while saying *"Stay!"* Your voice should be firm but gentle. It should *not* lilt upward as it would when you say your Rottweiler's name for attention. The hand signal is a quick, short motion from right to left with your fingers down, and palm toward the dog's nose.

• If your dog looks steady in his *sit,* take one step to the right leading with your right foot and following with your left. Repeat the *stay* command if you think your dog is going to move.

• After only two or three seconds away, return to your dog and give him the release command. Praise

Take one step away from your dog to test the "stay."

him quietly; you don't want him too wound up because you're going to practice this again.

• Continue practicing taking one step away until you feel your dog understands the *stay* command. You can build on this command by taking a step forward.

Hint: Always step out on the right foot when you want your dog to stay. The left foot will be a visual cue for your Rottweiler to follow you quickly as you progress to higher levels of training.

In a fenced area, take turns calling the Rottweiler from family member to family member, rewarding each "recall" with a treat and lots of praise and petting.

Eventually, you will be able to walk around your dog while he is on his *stay,* and later you can walk out to the end of the leash.

Always remember to reward your dog for a good *stay* with praise. If he begins to break his *stay,* say *"Ahh!"* and put him back into his *sit.* Praise him for a good *sit,* and then give him the *stay* command again. If he has broken his *stay,* back up your training to an easier level until he has mastered an easier *stay* before retrying a harder level.

Come

The *come* is definitely a command you'll want to teach your Rottweiler to obey—and every time you use it. However, this is the command that many dog owners of all breeds lament that their dogs never learn with any consistency. The rule of a good trainer is: If the dog isn't learning the task, then what is the trainer doing wrong? Remember: Bad training responses are not the dog's fault; the fault always lies in the manner in which the training is taught.

With this said, how do you teach a steady *come?*

• The first rule is to always make it fun! When you call your Rottweiler and he comes barreling toward you, praise him! Get excited! Make a fool of yourself. This rewards the Rottweiler for coming. Good things happen when he comes to you, too, like lots of attention, praise, and a really good treat.

• The second rule is to give the command when you know you will succeed. Say *"Come!"* when your puppy is running toward you anyway. Say *"Come!"* when your Rottweiler is on a leash and you are running backward. Your Rottweiler will come running toward you to play. You can also say *"Come!"* when your Rottweiler is on leash and you have something he really wants, like a favorite ball.

• As you progress with the *come* command, you can put your Rottweiler on a *sit-stay,* walk to the end of the leash, turn to face him, say his name, and then *"Come!"* Don't worry about making him sit in front of you just yet. You want to maintain that enthusiasm of a strong recall. If your Rottweiler does this exercise well, you can advance to a tracking or recall leash, which are roughly 30 feet (9 m) or so in length.

Two more final rules in teaching the *come* command:

1. Never punish your dog for coming when you call him. Often, owners make the mistake of punishing their dogs when they come. How can this happen? It can happen easily. The dog gets loose and the owner has been calling the dog *forever.* Finally, the Rottweiler decides, "O.K., I'll come now." Instead of forgetting the bad behavior—not coming when called—and immediately and enthusiastically rewarding and praising the dog when he *does* finally come, the owner is often tempted to punish the dog as soon as he is in reach. A Rottweiler has a mind like a steel trap. He won't forget this and he won't come next time. So, never

Command "come" as you run backwards and your Rottweiler follows.

mistakenly punish your dog for coming when you call him.

2. The other rule is to never test your dog's recall abilities off leash in open or unfenced areas. If your dog decides not to come, you have no way to encourage the correct response, as you would if the dog was on leash.

Walk Nicely

The key to training a dog to walk nicely on a leash is to begin early, before he starts pulling your arm out of the socket, and to keep the dog's attention. By nature, most Rottweilers are very attentive and will pay close attention to you. A dog that is hyperactive—one that lacks focus—can be very difficult to train. The Rottweiler is not meant to have this type of temperament or lack of focus, yet there are some dogs like this. If your Rottweiler has trouble focusing, it is even more important that you begin your leash work early. Once he reaches five months, you may have a difficult time recapturing his attention.

For those who own a Rottweiler with the classic working temperament and an eagerness to learn "what's next," a few simple tricks will help you to get your puppy walking on a leash nicely.

• First, be sure not to work on *walking nicely* on a leash when your dog

If your Rottweiler begins to go to your left, turn sharply to your right.

is bursting with energy and wants to play hard. Work off a little steam with a game of ball or fetch first.

• Once the energy edge is off your dog and he is ready to listen and work, attach the leash to his collar. Begin walking.

Hint: Start off with your Rottweiler on your left side and lead off with your left foot. As mentioned previously in this chapter, the left step will be a signal in higher levels of obedience for your dog to follow with you.

• If your puppy surges in front of you, turn an about-face and walk in the other direction. Encourage him to quickly follow you by saying his name and *"Hurry up! Hurry up!"*

• When he catches up, keep walking and tell him how good he is. Give him a little treat. If he wanders off to the right, turn left. If he trots to the left, turn right. Always be encouraging when he is turning toward you and catching up. Reward him when he is close by.

• If you see his mind is wandering and his body might follow, say his name, *"Schnitzel!"* in a pleasing, energetic way to get his attention back. Reward him with praise and treats.

Working in this manner while you're walking will be a challenge at first. You'll be turning everywhere and won't go anywhere in particular. Pretty soon your Rottweiler will catch on and will not drag you, lag behind you, or veer off to any side. He will pay attention to you and be by your side, which is a Rottweiler's favorite place.

Teaching Hand Signals

Rottweilers are eager to learn and are great fun to work with.

If you combine your voice command with a consistent hand signal, you will eventually be able to phase out the voice command and use strictly the hand signal. Unless you plan on competing in certain sports, you can use any hand signals you'd like. If, however, you want to participate in performance events, talk with trainers in these sports to find out what hand signals they prefer to use for the various commands. This way your Rottweiler has to learn the signals only once.

Chapter Fourteen

Beyond the Basics: Getting Involved

If you are interested in participating in activities with your Rottweiler, the good news is that your Rottweiler is so versatile she will be able to perform in a wide variety of activities. The bad news is that you won't have time for them all. There are worse fates in life for a dog owner, of course.

Consider Your Rottweiler's Strengths

When considering a sport for your Rottweiler, carefully consider the strengths of your dog. She will perform best in an activity for which she has special talents and one for which you enjoy training. Some Rottweilers are particularly adept at herding, others might excel at tracking, some enjoy carting, and most all are very good at obedience.

If you don't like competition, consider one of the many noncompetitive and community service activities in which the Rottweiler excels. If you're the outdoorsy type, you might consider working with your dog to

introduce her to backpacking. Rottweilers are good swimmers and if introduced to the water early and in a gentle way, often adore playing catch in the surf. As for community service work, Rottweilers frequently make exceptional animal-assisted therapy dogs and their work around the world as search and rescue dogs is legendary.

So, even if you've purchased your Rottweiler to be "just" a companion, don't let this limit you. Your Rottweiler *lives* to work and any of these activities will give her the opportunity to dazzle you with her intelligence and dedication.

Before You Begin

Before beginning any strenuous sports, it is important that your Rottweiler has fully matured and has received a complete veterinary physical. Rottweilers take longer to mature and are susceptible to some forms of injury, such as cruciate ligament tears (see page 134). Stressing a young dog's joints by participating in sports such as agility, which requires jumping and climbing, can also cause injuries. If you have any questions as to when you can begin

To compete successfully in conformation competition, your Rottweiler must possess excellent conformation and be shown by a person who is very skilled and polished in presenting the dog. This can either be you or a professional handler.

competing in an activity, consult with your veterinarian and other owners involved in the sport.

Competitive Activities for Rottweilers

If you thrive on the pressure and thrill of competition, there is a long list of sports in which you can work with your Rottweiler. Those owners who think they don't enjoy the stress of competition, should not overlook these sports before they've tried them. Often, the camaraderie in many sports takes much of the performance pressure off handlers.

The following is a list of sports in which the Rottweiler can and does perform well. Some may require special characteristics, for instance, conformation requires that a dog is close in form to the standard, while others require a combination of natural instincts and training.

Note: For information on sanctioning organizations for these activities, see Useful Addresses and Literature, page 159.

Agility

Agility is the fastest-growing dog sport in the United States. In agility,

The Rottweiler is a very versatile dog that can excel in a variety of competitive and noncompetitive activities.

the dog is off leash and is directed by the handler to navigate through a series of obstacles, including jumping over hurdles, weaving through poles, running over A-frames, trotting over a seesaw, and even running through a tunnel. The dog and handler with the fewest faults (points deducted for errors) and the fastest time wins.

Agility requires a Rottweiler that is mature—that is, at least two years old—and free of orthopedic problems. Agility clubs are popping up throughout the United States and it is generally not hard to find a group that is completely outfitted with a training facility and all the obstacles that are involved in the sport.

Agility is sanctioned by the American Kennel Club (AKC), North American Dog Agility Council (NADAC), and the United States Dog Agility Association (USDAA). Titles are awarded by each organization.

If you have an AKC-registered Rottweiler, you can enter agility events from all organizations. If your Rottweiler is adopted and does not have any papers, you can participate with an Indefinite Listing Privilege (ILP) number by applying in writing to AKC. Both NADAC and USDAA allow registered and unregistered Rottweilers to compete.

Conformation

We know your Rottweiler has the "brains," but does she have the "beauty?" Conformation is the only performance event in which looks count. In the show ring, your Rottweiler will be judged against the

Enthusiasm is key to a successful performance dog.

standard and against the other Rottweilers in the ring. The dog that is judged to be the best representative of the breed in the class wins. Winners from the various same sex classes, such as puppy, open bitch, bred by exhibitor, are then judged to choose a Winners Dog and a Winners Bitch. These winners receive championship points according to how many Rottweilers they beat in their respective sexes.

Then finally comes the battle for Best of Breed; eligibles include the "specials" or dogs that already have attained AKC championships, the Winners Dog, and Winners Bitch. These will compete for Best of Winners following selection of Best of Breed. Finally, one eligible dog is chosen for Best of Opposite Sex to Best of Breed. The breed winner goes on to compete in the Working

Group against the best of all these individual breeds. If a Rottweiler wins the Working Group, she would then move into the Best in Show competition.

Competing in conformation requires a lot of time, money, and travel. Amateur owner-handlers will need to polish their handling skills by either training under a knowledgeable handler or taking handling classes at a good training school. Many owners opt to hire a professional handler to show and travel with their Rottweilers.

Fun matches: If you are new to the breed, before you begin showing your dog you might want to enter some fun matches with local clubs to get some honest evaluations of your dog. Also, you can consult with your dog's breeder for another unbiased opinion. If your Rottweiler does seem to have what it takes to win in the show ring—near flawless conformation, a great temperament, and a flare for the show ring—by all means get involved. And keep in mind that if your Rottweiler doesn't win, she is performing in this event for *you* and she should always be number one with you in and out of the show ring.

Flyball

Flyball is a team sport and involves four dogs and handlers. The dogs perform in a relay that involves one dog at a time being sent down a 51-foot (15.5-m) course with four hurdles. At the end of the course, there is a box with a lever. The dog must hit the lever, which pops a tennis ball up into the air. The dog must catch the ball and race back over the hurdles to her handler where the next dog on the team is sent out. Winning teams are calculated by determining the fastest time minus any deductions for errors, such as running around a hurdle or dropping the ball.

The North American Flyball Association (NAFA) is the sanctioning organization for this event, and there are approximately 300 flyball clubs in the United States.

Herding

Rottweilers that excel in herding competitions tend to be those that are naturally very confident and have a strong desire to control and dominate stock. They are also the ones that are able to figure out on their own how to use the minimum amount of force necessary to achieve the job.

Herding requires natural instinct, focus, which is the ability of the dog to listen to her owner, obedience—the ability to respond to direction—and attitude, which is the ability to figure out what is the most efficient way to get things done. Rottweilers must be trained to develop their ability to herd through a lot of dedicated work and handling expertise. It is important to begin this sport with a young Rottweiler and train with an experienced herding club, particularly a club that is accustomed to the Rottweiler's herding style.

Herding competitions in which Rottweilers can compete are sanctioned by the AKC, American Herding Breed Association (AHBA), and the Australian Shepherd Club of America (ASCA). There's even an organization, the American Rottweiler Herding Fanciers, that publishes a newsletter and maintains a membership of owners of herding Rottweilers.

Musical Canine Freestyle

Musical canine freestyle is a sport in which dog and owner perform a choreographed routine to music.

There are two different sanctioning organizations for this sport: the Canine Freestyle Federation (CFF) and the World Canine Freestyle Organization (WCFO). Each organization has slightly different styles, rules, and regulations. In general, the sport requires an obedient Rottweiler, an owner with a little rhythm and coordination, and a desire to try something new. With both organizations, on- and off-leash events are offered, as well as entry-level classes for beginners.

Obedience

Virtually every Rottweiler and owner should be able to achieve a Companion Dog (CD) title from the AKC. To be awarded a CD, a Rottweiler must receive a passing score in three separate trials under three different judges. Exercises that are required for the CD title are
• Heel on leash and figure eight
• Stand for examination
• Heel free
• Recall
• Long *sit*
• Long *down*

If you and your Rottweiler achieve this title, you may be interested in pursuing additional titles, such as the Companion Dog Excellent (CDX) and Utility Dog (UD). Each level requires additional skills. For the CDX, the Rottweiler will be required to heel off leash, drop on recall, and perform retrieves on both the flat and over a jump. Utility Dog requirements include hand signals, scent discrimination, a directed retrieve, and a directed jump, as well as a moving stand and examination.

A recently added nonregular class is "rally-style obedience," which requires that the dog and handler—from the judge's *"Forward"*—go from station to station in the ring and

Whether your goal is to earn a "Companion Dog" degree, or to try for some of the more demanding obedience titles, your Rottweiler will benefit from the companionship and training.

perform the exercise that is listed at the station's sign. Exercises include jumps, changes in pace, spirals to left or right, about turns, and figure eights.

Schutzhund

Schutzhund is a dog sport that was begun in Germany as a test for a dog's aptitude for police work. Over the years it has developed into a family sport for all dogs. Schutzhund has classes for obedience and tracking, as well as for the all-round sport

dog, which involves obedience, tracking, and protection.

In the protection phase of Schutzhund, Rottweilers are trained to look for, bite, and hold a specially padded sleeve that is worn by a helper who poses as a "bad guy" in the tests.

If a Rottweiler is trained properly for the sport of Schutzhund, she will ignore anyone who is not wearing a sleeve. The protection phase is used mainly to determine the dog's ability to obey commands, think for her-

Taking part in Schutzhund trials requires a sound, steady temperament in a dog that can mentally and physically compete in obedience, tracking, and protection work.

self—she grabs the sleeve only *if* the helper moves—exhibit control—she must release the bite when told to—and work under stress.

Schutzhund is trained most effectively with positive reinforcement, such as treats, praise and toys, and play, even the protection phase. Rottweiler experts warn that any attempt to train this sport in a macho manner or using defensive training techniques will *not* work with the Rottweiler and should not be used.

Rottweiler owners interested in any of the offerings of Schutzhund should search hard for a training club that understands the Rottweiler and does not employ harsh training methods.

Tracking

Rottweilers can often make terrific tracking dogs; however, most trainers recommend beginning early.

The AKC offers three tracking titles: Tracking Dog (TD), Tracking Dog Excellent (TDX), and Variable Surface Tracking (VST). A Rottweiler that achieves all three titles is awarded a tracking championship, or Champion Tracker (CT). The tests are all pass/fail. Rottweilers may also participate in tracking through Schutzhund events which are competitive.

To become involved in tracking, look for local tracking clubs or contact your training school to see if they offer any tracking classes. If you have a Schutzhund club in your area, tracking will be taught through this club, too.

Noncompetitive Activities for Rottweilers

Backpacking

If you enjoy day hikes or camping, you might be interested in conditioning your Rottweiler for backpacking. This sport requires a dog that is in excellent physical shape and has no joint or heart problems. Backpacking also requires a well-fitted pack and some time to condition the Rottweiler to carrying a loaded pack that might weigh as much as one-third of her body weight. The Rottweiler also needs to learn the "width" of the pack to avoid getting it hung up on branches.

Rottweilers that are in training to backpack also need to learn to walk on a slack lead (the lead is attached to a clip on your belt, allowing the dog to lead you up the trail or follow), and be obedient enough not to chase after small game or deer; otherwise, you are in for quite a tumble.

For more information on training and conditioning a dog for backpacking, see Useful Addresses and Literature, page 164.

Canine Good Citizen

This AKC title is one that no Rottweiler should be without. It is a symbol of your dedication to your dog and excellent proof that your Rottweiler is well trained and sociable with both people and dogs. In the future, the CGC may very well be used by insurance companies to qualify homeowners for home insurance; for example, if your dog has the CGC, you are eligible for insurance no matter what breed you own.

The CGC involves ten tests that examine evidence of good care and such behavior components as your dog's acceptance of a friendly stranger, acceptance of another dog, sitting politely for petting, walking comfortably on a leash, people, and some basic obedience.

The test is offered to AKC-registered and nonregistered Rottweilers. It is a pass/fail test that is offered by training schools, 4-H centers, shelters, and even veterinary hospitals. Usually your local training school or shelter can tell you when the next test is scheduled in your area. These same organizations also offer training classes to help you prepare for the test. The only prerequisite for the test is that your Rottweiler be up to date on all her vaccinations.

Carting/Drafting/Driving

Pulling a cart is a skill the Rottweiler performed in Germany for centuries. Today, the Rottweiler can easily be taught to pull a cart and most dogs seem to really enjoy mastering this skill.

If you are interested in teaching your dog to cart (pull a cart with no rider), draft (pull a cart with a small load), or drive (pull a cart with a driver), you will need a wheeled vehicle, a good-fitting harness, and

someone who is experienced in this sport to help you train your dog. As with any strenuous exercise, your Rottweiler must have healthy joints and no heart disease. She should also be mature (two to three years old) to help avoid injuries.

Community Service Activities

The Rottweiler has a long history of serving mankind and has been a breed of choice for such community services as animal-assisted therapy and search and rescue. If you have the time and your Rottweiler has the talent, being able to serve your community by getting involved in one of these activities with your dog is tremendously gratifying.

Animal-assisted Therapy

The importance of animal-assisted therapy (AAT) is recognized by a wide range of settings, including rehabilitations hospitals, pediatric acute care facilities, long-term nursing care facilities, schools for the disabled, senior shut-in visitation programs, hospices, mental health facilities, abuse shelters, orphanages, and correctional facilities—to name just a few!

In order to become a certified AAT dog and handler team, you and your Rottweiler will most likely be required to attend a training class geared specifically toward training therapy dogs and practicing different scenarios, such as rolling wheel-

Rottweilers are among the most outstanding therapy dogs of all breeds.

chairs, loud noises, dropped pans, sudden movements, etc. In addition, some AAT organizations require the CGC certification from the AKC. Most AAT groups will administer their own therapy dog test and conduct an interview with both you and your Rottweiler present. Once you and your Rottweiler are certified in AAT, you may need to be recertified every few years, depending on the organization.

If you are considering pursuing AAT, visit a local training club to learn more about it. If you decide to proceed, you can begin the training and certification process. You can begin taking your Rottweiler to a good training school to learn the basics—*sit, stay, stand,* and *come,* and to work daily on good socialization skills with people. Dogs with nervous, fearful, or aggressive tendencies are not suitable for this work. The classic confident and tolerant Rottweiler temperament, however, is *superb* for AAT if combined with stellar training and excellent socialization.

Search and Rescue

When a child is lost in the woods or an Alzheimer patient has wandered away, time is of the essence and a good tracking or trailing dog is indispensable. Though some police and fire departments have dogs specifically trained for search and rescue (SAR), many more do not. In these cases, volunteer dog and handler teams are called in to help.

Though SAR teams are volunteers, they train with the seriousness and dedication of a full-time job. They are on call twenty-four hours a day, seven days a week. They use their own money to pay for gas and basic expenses, and sometimes travel hours by car. In some instances, SAR teams are flown in to help in searches across the country or even internationally. Large-scale searches might include searching collapsed buildings, either from a bombing or an earthquake. Sometimes the searches are for live victims; other times the search provides valuable closure to families mourning someone who didn't survive.

Without a doubt, SAR work is demanding physically and mentally for both dog and handler. It can also be dangerous at times. To become certified in SAR involves a lot of rigorous training and a series of tests. It's not easy, but it is extremely gratifying. If you own a Rottweiler that has good scenting abilities and is without any physical problems, this community service might be of interest to you.

To become involved in SAR, it is important that you find a good SAR club in your area. Meet with the members of this group and discuss what types of SAR they are involved in, how they train, when they meet, and what is expected of members. Additional information on SAR can be found in Useful Addresses and Literature, page 164.

Useful Addresses and Literature

Rottweiler Clubs

Note: Contact names change periodically. Please confirm current contacts through the ARC web site, or by calling the American Kennel Club.

American Rottweiler Club (ARC)
Corresponding Secretary: Pamela Grant
45 Erica Lane
Belen, MN 87002-2829
web site: *www.amrottclub.org*
Breeder Contact: Lauri Ladwig
1184 E. Fleetwood Court
Boise, ID 83706
(208) 424-1304

Rottweiler Rescue Foundation
Gwen Cheaney
(330) 722-3682

American Rottweiler Verein
Treasurer/Membership Director: Vesna Puharich
16450 Guyers Ford Drive
Boonville, Missouri 65233
(660) 882-9159
web site: *www.arv.org*

United States Rottweiler Club (USRC)
Corresponding Secretary: Leslie Fried
web site: *www.usrcweb.org*
e-mail: LFRotts@aol.com
Breed Rescue Affiliate: America Rescue the Rottweiler Foundation (ARRF)
Lala Roberts
914 Freestone
Arlington, TX 76017
(817) 466-3494 or (817) 937-3333

Allgemeiner Deutscher Rottweiler Klub (ADRK)
ADRK e.V.
Sudring 19
32429 Minden
Germany
(011) 49-571-50-40-40
web site: *www.bk-muenchen. de/english.htm*

All-Breed Registries

American Kennel Club
5580 Centerview Drive, Suite 200
Raleigh, North Carolina 27606-3390
(919) 233-3600
web site: *www.akc.org*

United Kennel Club
100 E. Kilgore Road
Kalamazoo, Michigan 49001-5598
(616) 343-9020
web site: *www.ukcdogs.com*

Rottweiler Rescue Groups

Note: There are many more regional and local Rottweiler rescue efforts currently being operated by exceptional Rottweiler breeders, trainers, and owners that are independently operated and not affiliated with a national breed club. Check with a local Rottweiler club, your veterinarian, or humane society for possible Rottweiler breed rescue contact information, or search the Internet for rescues in your area. A good starting point for finding many Rottweiler web sites can be accessed at: *www.msu.edu/~silvar/arottlinks.htm*

Rottweiler Breed Rescue
ARC Rottweiler Rescue Foundation
(see ARC listing)

America Rescue the Rottweiler
   Foundation
(see USRC listing)

Los Angeles Rottweiler Rescue
Beverly Silvar, President
(818) 765-5997
web site: *www.msu.edu/~silvar/beverly.htm*

MidAmerica Rottweiler Rescue
Elizabeth Davies, President
P.O. Box 45743
Omaha, Nebraska 68127

web site: *www.adoptarott.org*
e-mail: elizabeth@adoptarrott.org

Southern States Rottweiler Rescue
JoRett B. Redman, President
(205) 487-5500
web site: *www.ssrottweilerrescue.org*
e-mail: vschwerd@sonet.net

Wisconsin Rottweiler Rescue
Joan Sweeney, President
3617 S. Dutch Mill Road
Madison, Wisconsin 53718
(608) 224-0272
web site: *www.wirottrescue.f2s.com*
e-mail: joan.sweeney@finaids.wisc.edu

Activities

Agility
See American Kennel Club listing.

North American Dog Agility Council
   (NADAC)
HRC2, Box 277
St. Maries, ID 83861
Fax: (208) 689-3906
web site: *www.nadac.com*
e-mail: nadack9@aol.com

United States Dog Agility
   Association (USDAA)
P.O. Box 850955
Richardson, TX 75085
(214) 231-9700
web site: *www.usdaa.com*

Be sure to work with your Rottweiler regularly to make sure she is reliable with people of all ages.

Animal Assisted Therapy
The Delta Society
289 Perimeter Road East
Renton, Washington 98055-1329
(800) 869-6898
web site: *ww.deltasociety.com*

Therapy Dogs International, Inc.
88 Bartley Road
Flanders, New Jersey 07836
(973) 252-9800
web site: *www.tdi_dog.org*

Canine Good Citizen
Canine Good Citizen Department
American Kennel Club
5580 Centerview Dr.
Raleigh, NC 27606
(919) 852-3875
web site: *www.akc.org/love/cgc/*
index.cfm

Conformation
See American Kennel Club listing.
web site: *http://www.akc.org/dic/*
events/conform/index.cfm

See United States Rottweiler Club
and American Rottweiler Verein
listings.

Flyball
North American Flyball Association
(NAFA)
1400 Devon Ave.
Box 512
Chicago, IL 60660
web site: *www.flyball.org*

Herding
See American Kennel Club listing.

American Herding Breed
Association (AHBA)
Lea Allen
AHBA Membership Coordinator
277 Central Ave.
Seekonk, MA 02771
(508) 761-4078
web site: *www.primenet.com/*
~joell/ahba/main.htm
e-mail: pecans@ix.netcom.com

Australian Shepherd Club of
American (ASCA)
P.O. Box 3790
Bryan, TX 77805-3790
(800) 892-ASCA; (979) 778-1082
web site: *www.asca.org*
e-mail: lola@asca.org

Musical Canine Freestyle
Canine Freestyle Federation
Monica Patty, Corresponding
Secretary
21900 Foxden Lane
Leesburg, Virginia 20175
(703) 327-4860
web site: *www.caninefreestyle.org*
e-mail: secretary@canine-freestyle.
org
mailing list: *http://onelist.com/*
community/CFFCanine

FreestyleWorld Canine Freestyle
Organization
P.O. Box 350122
Brooklyn, NY 11235
(718) 332-8336
web site: *www.woofs.org/wcfo/*

This original acrylic by Cedric Hustace presents an interesting grouping, including (l-r) the author, her translator Heinrich Mörtl, Gabriele Tenscher with her dog, of Augsburg, Germany, Rottweiler breeder and trainer Franz Menacher of Landsberg, Germany, and Curtis Hustace, the photographer who provided most of the illustrations in this book.

e-mail: wcfodogs@aol.com
mailing list: worldcaninefreestyle-
  subscribe@egroups.com

Obedience
See American Kennel Club listing.
web site: *www.akc.org/dic/events/
  obedtrack/akcobed.cfm*

See United Kennel Club listing.
web site: *www.ukcdogs.com/
  obedience.html*

Association of Pet Dog Trainers
  (APDT)
P.O. Box 385
Davis, CA 95617
(800) 738-3647
web site: *www.apdt.com*

National Association of Dog
  Obedience Instructors
  (NADOI)
Attn: Suzi Bluford, Corresponding
  Secretary
PMB #369
729 Grapevine Hwy, Suite 369
Hurst, TX 76054-2085
web site: *www.nadoi.org*
e-mail: suzibluf@aol.com

Schutzhund
DVG America
Secretary: Sandi Prudy
5718 Watson Circle
Dallas, TX 75225
web site: *http://webusers.anet-stl.
  com/~dvgamer*

United Schutzhund Clubs of
America
3810 Paule Avenue
St. Louis, Missouri
(314) 638-9686
e-mail: usaschutzhund@worldnet.
att.net

See USRC and ARV listings.

Search and Rescue
American Rescue Dog Association
P.O. Box 151
Chester, NY 10918
web site: *www.ardainc.org*

Tracking
See American Kennel Club listing.
web site: *www.akc.org/dic/events/
obedtrack/trackreg.cfm*

See Schutzhund listing.

Books

Activities
Agility: Simmons-Moake, Jane.
*Agility Training, the Fun Sport for
All Dogs.* New York: Howell Book
House, 1992.
Animal-assisted Therapy: Burch,
Mary R., and Aaron Honori
Katcher. *Volunteering with Your
Pet: How to Get Involved in Ani-
mal-Assisted Therapy with Any
Kind of Pet.* New York: Howell
Book House, 1996.
Davis, Kathy Diamond. *Therapy
Dogs: Training Your Dog to
Reach Others.* New York: Howell
Book House, 1992.

Backpacking: LaBelle, Charlene. *A
Guide to Backpacking with Your
Dog.* Loveland, CO: Alpine Publi-
cations, 1992.
Canine Good Citizen: Volhard,
Jack, and Wendy Volhard. *The
Canine Good Citizen: Every Dog
Can Be One,* 2nd edition. New
York: Howell Book House, 1997.
Conformation: Coile, Caroline D.
Show Me! A Dog Show Primer.
Hauppauge, NY: Barron's Edu-
cational Series, Inc., 1997.
Hall, Lynn. *Dog Showing for Begin-
ners.* New York: Howell Book
House, 1994.
Stern, Jane, and Michael Stern.
*Dog Eat Dog: A Very Human
Book about Dogs and Dog
Shows.* New York: Simon &
Schuster Trade, 1998.
Flyball: Olson, Lonnie. *Flyball Rac-
ing: The Dog Sport for Everyone.*
New York: Macmillan General
Reference, 1997.
Obedience: Bauman, Diane.
Beyond Basic Dog Training. New
York: Howell Book House, 1991.
Handler, Barbara. *Successful Obe-
dience Handling: The New Best
Foot Forward.* Loveland, CO:
Alpine Publications, Inc., 1991.
Schutzhund: Barwig, Susan.
*Schutzhund: Theory and Training
Methods.* New York: Howell
Book House, 1991.
Search and Rescue: American
Dog Rescue Association. *Search
and Rescue Dogs: Training
Methods.* New York: Howell
Book House, 1991.

Will this puppy be a future champion? Or, perhaps, an agility whiz? Time will tell, but a good breeder can also help you select a puppy that is most likely to meet your needs.

Tracking: Brown, Tom. *The Science and Art of Tracking.* New York: Penguin USA, 1999.

Sanders, William. *Enthusiastic Tracking: The Step-by-Step Training Handbook.* Stanwood, WA: Rime Publications, 1998.

Health

American Animal Hospital Association with Sally Borewell and Alan Dubowy. *American Animal Hospital Association Encyclopedia of Dog Health and Care.* New York: Morrow, William & Co., 1996.

Hoffman, Matthew, and Lowell J. Ackerman, Editors. *Dogs: The Ultimate Care Guide.* Emmaus, Pennsylvania: Rodale Press, 2000.

Siegel, Mordecai, and University of California-Davis, School of Veterinary Medicine Faculty and Staff. *UC Davis Book of Dogs:*

A Complete Medical Reference Guide for Dogs & Puppies. New York: HarperCollins, 1995.

Rottweilers

Brace, Andrew H., Editor. *The Ultimate Rottweiler.* New York: Howell Book House, 1995.

Forster, Jean. *The Rottweiler: An Owner's Guide to a Happy, Healthy Pet.* New York: Howell Book House, 1995.

Freeman, Muriel. *The Complete Rottweiler.* New York: Howell Book House, 1984.

McNinch, Barbara L. *Training Your Rottweiler.* Hauppauge, NY: Barron's Educational Series, Inc., 1999.

Training

General Training: Dunbar, Ian. *How to Teach a New Dog Old Tricks,* 2nd edition. Oakland, CA: James and Kenneth Publishers, 1991.

Pryor, Karen. *Don't Shoot the Dog.* Waltham, MA: Sunshine Books, 1984.

Head Halter Training: Fields-Babineau, Miriam. *Dog Training with a Head Halter.* Hauppauge, NY: Barron's Educational Series, Inc., 2000.

House-training: Kalstone, Shirlee. *How to Housebreak Your Dog in 7 Days.* New York: Bantam Books, 1985.

The key to being a successful Rottweiler owner is to understand the basic nature of this wonderful breed, and maintain the dominant position in your "pack."

Index